LSAT Hacks

LSAT Preptest 74 Explanations

A Study Guide for LSAT 74
(December 2014 LSAT)

Graeme Blake

ISBN 13: 978-1-927997-09-3
ISBN 10: 1-927997-09-7

Testimonials

Self-study is my preferred way to prep, but I often felt myself missing a few questions each test. Especially for Logic Games, I wanted to see those key inferences which I just couldn't seem to spot on my own. That's where *LSAT Hacks* came in. These solutions have been a tremendous help for my prep, and in training myself to think the way an experienced test taker would.

- Spencer B.

Graeme paraphrases the question in plain terms, and walks through each step in obtaining the right answer in a very logical way. This book uses the same techniques as other guides, but its so much more consistent and concise! By the time you read through all the tests, you've gradually developed your eye for the questions. Using this book is a great way to test your mastery of techniques!

- Sara L.

Graeme's explanations have the most logical and understandable layout I've seen in an LSAT prep book. The explanations are straightforward and easy to understand, to the point where they make you smack your forehead and say 'of course!

- Michelle V.

"Graeme is someone who clearly demonstrates not only LSAT mastery, but the ability to explain it in a compelling manner. This book is an excellent addition to whatever arsenal you're amassing to tackle the LSAT."

- J.Y. Ping, 7Sage LSAT,
www.7Sage.com

I did not go through every single answer but rather used the explanations to see if they could explain why my answer was wrong and the other correct. I thought the breakdown of "Type", "Conclusion", "Reasoning" and "Analysis" was extremely useful in simplifying the question. As for quality of the explanations I'd give them a 10 out of 10.

- Christian F.

LSAT PrepTests come with answer keys, but it isn't sufficient to know whether or not you picked the credited choice to any given question. The key to making significant gains on this test is understanding the logic underlying the questions.

This is where Graeme's explanations really shine. You may wonder whether your reasoning for a specific question is sound. For the particularly challenging questions, you may be at a complete loss as to how they should be approached.

Having these questions explained by Graeme who scored a 177 on the test is akin to hiring an elite tutor at a fraction of the price. These straightforward explanations will help you improve your performance and, more fundamentally, enhance your overall grasp of the test content.

- Morley Tatro, Cambridge LSAT,
www.cambridgelsat.com

Through his conversational tone, helpful introductions, and general recommendations and tips, Graeme Blake has created an enormously helpful companion volume to *The Next Ten Actual Official LSATs*. He strikes a nice balance between providing the clarity and basic explanation of the questions that is needed for a beginner and describing the more complicated techniques that are necessary for a more advanced student.

Even though the subject matter can be quite dry, Graeme succeeds in making his explanations fun and lighthearted. This is crucial: studying for the LSAT is a daunting and arduous task. By injecting some humor and keeping a casual tone, the painful process of mastering the LSAT becomes a little less painful.

When you use *LSAT Hacks* in your studying, you will feel like you have a fun and knowledgeable tutor guiding you along the way.

- Law Schuelke, LSAT Tutor,
www.lawLSAT.com

Graeme's explanations are clear, concise and extremely helpful. They've seriously helped me increase my understanding of the LSAT material!

- **Jason H.**

Graeme's book brings a different view to demystifying the LSAT. The book not only explains the right and wrong answers, but teaches you how to read the reading comprehension and the logical reasoning questions. His technique to set up the games rule by rule help me not making any fatal mistakes in the set up. The strategies he teaches can be useful for someone starting as much as for someone wanting to perfect his strategies. Without his help my LSAT score would have been average, he brought my understanding of the LSAT and my score to a higher level even if english is not my mother tongue.

- **Patrick Du.**

This book is a must buy for any who are looking to pass or improve their LSAT, I highly recommend it.

- **Patrick Da.**

This book was really useful to help me understand the questions that I had more difficulty on. When I was not sure as to why the answer to a certain question was that one, the explanations helped me understand where and why I missed the right answer in the first place. I recommend this book to anyone who would like to better understand the mistakes they make.

- **Pamela G.**

Graeme's book is filled with thoughtful and helpful suggestions on how to strategize for the LSAT test. It is well-organized and provides concise explanations and is definitely a good companion for LSAT preparation.

- **Lydia L.**

The explanations are amazing, great job. I can hear your voice in my head as I read through the text.

- **Shawn M.**

LSAT Hacks, especially the logic games sections, was extremely helpful to my LSAT preparation.

The one downside to self study is that sometimes we do not know why we got a question wrong and thus find it hard to move forward. Graeme's book fixes that; it offers explanations and allows you to see where you went wrong. This is an extremely helpful tool and I'd recommend it to anybody that's looking for an additional study supplement.

- **Joseph C.**

Regardless of how well you're scoring on the LSAT, this book is very helpful. I used it for LR and RC. It breaks down and analyzes each question without the distraction of classification and complicated methods you'll find in some strategy books. Instead of using step-by-step procedures for each question, the analyses focus on using basic critical thinking skills and common sense that point your intuition in the right direction. Even for questions you're getting right, it still helps reinforce the correct thought process. A must-have companion for reviewing prep tests.

- **Christine Y.**

Take a thorough mastery of the test, an easygoing demeanor, and a genuine desire to help, and you've got a solid resource for fine-tuning your approach when you're tirelessly plowing through test after test. Written from the perspective of a test-taker, this book should help guide your entire thought process for each question, start to finish.

- **Yoni Stratievsky, Harvard Ready,** www.harvardready.com

This LSAT guide is the best tool I could have when preparing for the LSAT. Not only does Graeme do a great job of explaining the sections as a whole, he also offers brilliant explanations for each question. He takes the time to explain why an answer is wrong, which is far more helpful when trying to form a studying pattern.

- **Amelia F.**

LSAT 74 Explanations
Table Of Contents

Introduction

The LSAT is a hard test.

The only people who take the LSAT are smart people who did well in University. The LSAT takes the very best students, and forces them to compete.

If the test's difficulty shocked you, this is why. The LSAT is a test designed to be hard for smart people.

That's the bad news. But there's hope. The LSAT is a *standardized* test. It has patterns. It can be learned.

To get better, you have to review your mistakes. Many students write tests and move on, without fully understanding their mistakes.

This is understandable. The LSAC doesn't publish official explanations for most tests. It's hard to be sure why you were wrong.

That's where this book comes in. It's a companion for LSAT 74, the December 2014 LSAT.

This book lets you see where you went wrong. It has a full walk through of each question and of every answer choice. You can use this book to fix your mistakes, and make sure you understand *everything*.

By getting this book, you've shown that you're serious about beating this test. I sincerely hope it helps you get the score you want.

There are a few things that I'd like to highlight.

Logical Reasoning: It can be hard to identify conclusions in LR. You don't get feedback on whether you identified the conclusion correctly.

This book gives you that feedback. I've identified the conclusion and the reasoning for each argument. Try to find these on your own beforehand, and make sure they match mine.

Logic Games: Do the game on your own before looking at my explanation. You can't think about a game unless you're familiar with the rules. Once you read my explanations, draw my diagrams yourself on a sheet of paper. You'll understand them much better by recopying them.

Reading Comprehension: You should form a mental map of the passage. This helps you locate details quickly. Make a 1-2 line summary of each paragraph (it can be a mental summary).

I've written my own summaries for each passage. They show the minimum amount of information that you should know after reading a passage, without looking back.

I've included line references in my explanations. You do not need to check these each time. They're only there in case you aren't sure where something is.

Do these three things, and you can answer most Reading Comprehension questions with ease.:

1. Know the point of the passage.
2. Understand the passage, in broad terms. Reread anything you don't understand.
3. Know where to find details. That's the point of the paragraph summaries. I usually do mine in my head, and they're shorter than what I've written.

Review This Book

Before we start, I'd like to ask you a favor. I'm an independent LSAT instructor. I don't have a marketing budget.

But I do my best to make good guides to the LSAT. If you agree, I would love it if you took two minutes to write a review on amazon.com

People judge a book by its reviews. So if you like this guide you can help others discover it. I'd be very grateful.

Good luck!

Graeme

p.s. I'm a real person, and I want to know how the LSAT goes and what you think of this book. Send me an email at graeme@lsathacks.com!

p.p.s. For more books, check out the further reading section at the back. I'm also offering a free half hour LSAT lesson if you fill out a survey.

How To Use This Book

The word "Hacks" in the title is meant in the sense used by the tech world and Lifehacker: "solving a problem" or "finding a better way".

The LSAT can be beaten, but you need a good method. My goal is for you to use this book to understand your mistakes and master the LSAT.

This book is *not* a replacement for practicing LSAT questions on your own.

You have to try the questions by yourself first. When you review, try to see why you were wrong *before* you look at my explanations.

Active review will teach you to fix your own mistakes. The explanations are there for when you have difficulty solving on a question on your own or when you want another perspective on a question.

When you *do* use the explanations, have the question on hand. These explanations are not meant to be read alone. You should use them to help you think about the questions more deeply.

Most of the logical reasoning explanations are pretty straightforward. Necessary assumption questions are often an exception, so I want to give you some guidance to help you interpret the explanations.

The easiest way to test the right answer on a necessary assumption question is to "negate" it.

You negate a statement by making it false, in the slightest possible way. For example, the negation of "The Yankees will win all their games" is "The Yankees will *not* win all their games (they will lose at least one)."

You *don't* have to say that the Yankees will lose *every* game. That goes too far.

If the negation of an answer choice proves the conclusion wrong, then that answer is *necessary* to the argument, and it's the correct answer.

Often, I negate the answer choices when explaining necessary assumption questions, so just keep in mind why they're negated.

Logic games also deserve special mention.

Diagramming is a special symbolic language that you have to get comfortable with to succeed.

If you just *look* at my diagrams without making them yourself, you may find it hard to follow along. You can only learn a language by using it yourself.

So you will learn *much* more if you draw the diagrams on your own. Once you've seen how I do a setup, try to do it again by yourself.

With constant practice, you *will* get better at diagramming, and soon it will come naturally.

But you must try on your own. Draw the diagrams.

Note that when you draw your own diagrams, you don't have to copy every detail from mine. For example, I often leave off the numbers when I do linear games. I've included them in the book, because they make it easier for you to follow along.

But under timed conditions, I leave out many details so that I can draw diagrams faster. If you practice making drawings with fewer details, they become just as easy to understand.

Keep diagrams as minimal as possible.

If you simply don't *like* the way I draw a certain rule type, then you can substitute in your own style of diagram. Lots of people succeed using different styles of drawing.

Just make sure your replacement is easy to draw consistently, and that the logical effect is the same. I've chosen these diagrams because they are clear, they're easy to draw, and they *keep you from forgetting rules*.

I've included line references to justify Reading Comprehension Answers. Use these only in case you're unsure about an explanation. You don't have to go back to the passage for every line reference.

Short Guide to Logical Reasoning

LR Question Types

Must be True: The correct answer is true.

Most Strongly Supported: The correct answer is probably true.

Strengthen/Weaken: The answer is correct if it even slightly strengthens/weakens the argument.

Parallel Reasoning: The correct answer will mirror the argument's structure exactly. It is often useful to diagram these questions (but not always).

Sufficient Assumption: The correct answer will prove the conclusion. It's often useful to diagram sufficient assumption questions. For example:

The conclusion is: A → D

There is a gap between premises and conclusion:

A   B → C → D   **missing link:** A → B or B̶ → A̶

A → B → C   D   **missing link:** C → D or D̶ → C̶

A → B   C → D   **missing link:** B → C or C̶ → B̶

The right answer will provide the missing link.

Necessary Assumption: The correct answer will be essential to the argument's conclusion. Use the negation technique: If the correct answer is false (negated), then the argument falls apart.
The negation of hot is "not hot" rather than cold.

Here's how to do negations: You just make the idea false. This is not so much about grammar as it is about thinking what the idea is, and a counterexample. E.g.

"All Americans are nice" → "One guy in Arkansas named Bob is sort of mean. Every single other American is always really nice"

The "grammatical" negation is "not all Americans are nice", but it's so much clearer and easier to think in terms of making the idea not true.

Point at Issue: Point at Issue questions require two things. **1.** The two speakers must express an opinion on something. **2.** They must disagree about it.

Flawed Reasoning: The correct answer will be a description of a reasoning error made in the argument. It will often be worded very abstractly.

Practice understanding the answers, right and wrong. Flawed Reasoning answers are very abstract, but they all mean something. Think of examples to make them concrete and easier to understand.

Basic Logic

Take the phrase: "All cats have tails."

"Cats" is the sufficient condition. Knowing that something is a cat is "sufficient" for us to say that it has a tail. "Tails" is a necessary condition, because you can't be a cat without a tail. You can draw this sentence as C → T

The **contrapositive** is a correct logical deduction, and reads "anything without a tail is not a cat." You can draw this as T̶ → C̶. Notice that the terms are reversed, and negated.

Incorrect Reversal: "Anything with a tail is a cat." This is a common logical error on the LSAT.

T → C   (Wrong! Dogs have tails and aren't cats.)

Incorrect Negation: "If it is not a cat, it doesn't have a tail." This is another common error.

C̶ → T̶ (Wrong! Dogs aren't cats, but have tails.)

General Advice: Always remember what you are looking for on each question. The correct answer on a strengthen question would be incorrect on a weaken question.

Watch out for subtle shifts in emphasis between the stimulus and the incorrect answer choices. An example would be the difference between "how things are" and "how things should be."

Justify your answers. If you're tempted to choose an answer choice that says something like the sentence below, then be sure you can fill in the blank:

Answer Choice Says: "The politician attacked his opponents' characters",

Fill In The Blank: "The politician said _____ about his opponents' characters."

If you cannot say what the attack was, you can't pick that answer. This applies to many things. You must be able to show that the stimulus supports your idea.

A Few Logic Games Tips

Rule 1: When following along with my explanations....draw the diagrams yourself, too!

This book will be much more useful if you try the games by yourself first. You must think through games on your own, and no book will do that for you. You must have your mind in a game to solve it.

Use the explanations when you find a game you can't understand on your own, or when you want to know how to solve a game more efficiently.

Some of the solutions may seem impossible to get on your own. It's a matter of practice. When you learn how to solve one game efficiently, solving other games becomes easier too.

Try to do the following when you solve games:

Work With What Is Definite: Focus on what must be true. Don't figure out every possibility.

Draw Your Deductions: Unsuccessful students often make the same deductions as successful students. But the unsuccessful students forget their deductions, 15 seconds later! I watch this happen.

Draw your deductions, or you'll forget them. Don't be arrogant and think this doesn't happen to you. It would happen to *me* if I didn't draw my deductions.

Draw Clear Diagrams: Many students waste time looking back and forth between confusing pictures. They've done everything right, but can't figure out their own drawings!

You should be able to figure out your drawings 3 weeks later. If you can't, then they aren't clear enough. I'm serious: look back at your old drawings. Can you understand them? If not, you need a more consistent, cleaner system.

Draw Local Rules: When a question gives you a new rule (a local rule), draw it. Then look for deductions by combining the new rule with your existing rules. Then double-check what you're being asked and see if your deduction is the right answer. This works 90% of the time for local rule questions. And it's fast.

If you don't think you have time to draw diagrams for each question, practice drawing them faster. It's a learnable skill, and it pays off.

Try To Eliminate a Few Easy Answer Choices First: You'll see examples in the explanations that show how certain deductions will quickly get rid of 1-3 answer choices on many questions. This saves time for harder answer choices and it frees up mental space.

You don't have to try the answer choices in order, without thinking about them first.

Split Games Into Two Scenarios When Appropriate: If a rule only allows something to be one of two ways (e.g. F is in 1 or 7), then draw two diagrams: one with F in 1, and one with F in 7. This leads to extra deductions surprisingly often. And it always makes the game easier to visualize.

Combine Rules To Make Deductions: Look for variables that appear in multiple rules. These can often be combined. Sometimes there are no deductions, but it's a crime not to look for them.

Reread The Rules: Once you've made your diagram, reread the rules. This lets you catch any mistakes, which are fatal. It doesn't take very long, and it helps you get more familiar with the rules.

Draw Rules Directly On The Diagram: Mental space is limited. Three rules are much harder to remember than two. When possible, draw rules on the diagram so you don't have to remember them.

Memorize Your Rules: You should memorize every rule you can't draw on the diagram. It doesn't take long, you'll go faster, and you'll make fewer mistakes. Try it, it's not that hard.

If you spend 30 seconds doing this, you'll often save a minute by going through the game faster.

You should also make a numbered list of rules that aren't on the diagram, in case you need to check them.

Section I – Logical Reasoning

Question 1

QUESTION TYPE: Complete the Argument

CONCLUSION: Jones' books prevent students from enjoying more complex books.

REASONING: Jones' books are like candy. They create short term excitement, but prevent you from liking better food.

ANALYSIS: This is an argument by analogy. To predict the answer, you should think about what the analogy says. The point of the analogy is that we like candy in the short term, but it's better to eat real food in the long run. The same is therefore true of Jones' books vs. real literature.

The question uses complex language. For example, "fare" instead of "food". When you come across hard words, don't panic. Read around them for context. Start with words you know, and use them to understand the others. You don't need to understand words perfectly to get a question right.

Then flag the question for review. On review look up every word you don't know. This is how people with large vocabularies learn more words – we're always using dictionaries. If you're using a Mac, type cmd + space to bring up Finder, then type the word to search for it in the excellent dictionary app.

———————

A. Candy is just an analogy. Books won't make you eat sweets.
B. Jones' books are like candy, so they're *easy* to read. The problem is that you won't want to read anything harder.
C. **CORRECT.** The problem with candy is that it dulls our taste for real food. The author says Jones' books are like candy, so this answer finishes their thought.
D. The argument doesn't even mention parents. The author didn't say *who* should discourage children. Maybe teachers are the ones able to stop them from reading Jones' books.
E. This doesn't match the analogy. The author didn't say that people spend all their time eating once they get a taste for candy.

Question 2

QUESTION TYPE: Strengthen

CONCLUSION: The Parthenon's stonemasons may have used a drawing similar to the one found at Didyma.

REASONING: At Didyma, there is a drawing in a temple which shows the correct width of a column using a grid.

ANALYSIS: The archaeologist is trying to figure out how the stonemasons calculated the width of the columns at the Parthenon.

The only evidence is a drawing that *could* have been used to measure widths. The fact that something *could have been* used by architects doesn't mean that drawings were *actually* used by architects. We can strengthen this argument by supporting the idea that Greeks used drawings when constructing buildings.

———————

A. This actually *weakens* the argument, a little. Modern architects use drawings. If such a method fails to recreate the Parthenon, then maybe the ancients had other methods.
B. This weakens the argument. It raises the possibility that architectural drawing was only developed after the Parthenon was built.
C. **CORRECT.** This supports the argument by showing that drawings indeed were used for construction.
D. So? The author wasn't saying the Didyma drawings were used to construct the Parthenon. Their implied argument was that a similar but different drawing would have been used at the Parthenon.
E. The fact that the architects were experienced doesn't explain *how* they carved columns.

Question 3

QUESTION TYPE: Principle

CONCLUSION: The government shouldn't use lottery revenue to fund health care.

REASONING: Lottery revenue might decline. Health care is essential.

ANALYSIS: The author is arguing that health services are necessary and lottery revenues are uncertain. The underlying premise is that essential services should only be funded from stable revenue sources.

A. The argument wasn't talking about how to spend money. The argument was instead about *which* money to use for spending that is already planned (health spending).
B. **CORRECT.** If this weren't true, then the argument wouldn't make sense. The only reason lottery funding is unsuitable for health care is because health care is essential.
C. We don't even know if this is true. The author said that lottery money is unsuitable for health care because health care is essential. But maybe some less essential services could be funded from the lottery.
D. The author didn't say what governments should think. The author's argument is that health is essential, and it doesn't matter if governments agree or not.
E. This just randomly combines two concepts from the stimulus. In the stimulus, lotteries were mentioned as the *cause* of shortfalls. Maybe some money should be set aside, but that has nothing to do with the proper source of funding for healthcare.

Question 4

QUESTION TYPE: Strengthen

CONCLUSION: Heated squirrel tails help California ground squirrels deter rattlesnake attacks.

REASONING: The tails of California ground squirrels heat up when squirrels defend against rattlesnake attacks. Rattlesnakes can see heat with infrared sensing.

ANALYSIS: This argument is far less persuasive than it sounds. If you move your arm, it heats up. That doesn't mean your arm's heat is a defense mechanism against rattlesnake attacks.

This argument has shown that it's *possible* that the heat in squirrel tails helps them defend against rattlesnake attacks. To strengthen the argument, we need to show actual evidence that heated tails serve a purpose.

A. Who cares about rattlesnake tails? The question is about squirrel tails.
B. This answer is useless. It's not surprising that squirrels use their tails for multiple purposes. This doesn't help us prove anything about the effect squirrel tails have on rattlesnakes.
C. **CORRECT.** This supports the argument by actually isolating heat as a factor. It shows that heated tails deter rattlesnakes better than regular tails do.
D. It doesn't matter what squirrels do with other predators. The argument is about heat and rattlesnakes. This answer doesn't even mention heat; it's a distraction.
E. Who cares? Rattlesnakes *do* have an organ to sense infrared energy, and they're the ones we're concerned with.

Question 5

QUESTION TYPE: Flawed Reasoning

CONCLUSION: Fillmore is wrong.

REASONING: Fillmore's argument benefits Fillmore.

ANALYSIS: This question makes an ad hominem flaw. The author notes that, as a television executive, Fillmore stands to benefit if very young children watch TV.

It's fine to point out a conflict of interest. But that can't be your entire argument: a conflict of interest proves nothing on its own. The critic didn't show any evidence that Fillmore is actually wrong.

_____

A. This didn't happen.
   Example of flaw: Fillmore said that children can benefit from TV (TV → B). Therefore, Fillmore argued that only TV is beneficial for children (B → TV).
B. This is a different flaw.
   Example of flaw: Fillmore said that TV is fine because there's no evidence that it's bad.
C. **CORRECT.** This correctly describes an ad hominem flaw.
D. This is a different flaw.
   Example of flaw: TV is bad for children. My uncle Sam said so. He never had children, and he has never watched TV. But he's pretty smart, so he must be right.
E. This is a different flaw. It's *very* rare for an author to contradict themselves. In fact, this is so rare that it's hard to come up with an example.
   Example of flaw: John says that dogs are the best pets and that cats are even better pets than dogs.

Question 6

QUESTION TYPE: Weaken

CONCLUSION: We should take lower doses of medicines combined with grapefruit juice.

REASONING: A chemical in grapefruit juice increases the effect of medicines. It's always best to take the smallest dose of medicine that will produce the desired effect.

ANALYSIS: Medical doses need to be precise. This argument tells us that grapefruit juice increases the effect of medicine. It doesn't tell us *how much* the effect is increased, or if it's constant for all medicines or for all quantities of grapefruit juice.

We have two options:

1. Rigorously test the right amount of grapefruit juice for all medicines, and make sure that patients take *exactly* that quantity with the right amount of chemical.
2. Tell patients to avoid grapefruit juice.

Hmm, which is simpler.....?

_____

A. **CORRECT.** This destroys the argument. Medical doses require precision. If we can't be sure of the quantity of the chemical, then it's impossible to predict the effect of grapefruit juice on medicines.
B. This supports the argument. It provides an additional reason for replacing medicine with grapefruit juice.
C. This just confirms that the chemical has an effect. But this information is irrelevant to the argument. The author said that we should give patients grapefruit juice *with* the chemical in order to reduce the required amount of medicine.
D. This is just a random fact about how the chemical works. It has no impact on the argument.
E. This tells us that doctors were aware that grapefruit juice had an effect before they knew why it had an effect. That's an interesting fact, but it has nothing to do with whether patients should follow the radical course of action outlined in the stimulus.

Question 7

QUESTION TYPE: Principle

CONCLUSION: The landlord should buy the FreezAll instead of the Sno-Queen.

REASONING: Both machines are the same price. Both meet the landlord's needs. The FreezAll is less powerful.

ANALYSIS: The two machines are identical, except that the FreezAll is less powerful while still meeting the landlord's needs.

Clearly, the principle is that consumers should choose the less powerful machine that still works for them. There may be good reasons for doing this. Perhaps more powerful machines are more likely to break down or require more expensive maintenance.

_____

A. This is ridiculous. If an answer is an insane statement that no one in real life would agree with, it won't be the right answer.
For instance, imagine a chocolate bar that contains traces of nuts compared to an identically priced bar that doesn't. This principle says that either product will meet the needs of someone with a nut allergy, because the prices are the same.
B. This *contradicts* what the saleswoman said! Both units are the same price, yet the saleswoman recommends the less powerful product.
C. This principle has no effect. Both products are the same price, so we can't say which has better value.
D. This is an unethical principle, and highly unlikely to be the right answer. But more to the point, the stimulus didn't mention commissions or whether the commission between the two items is different.
E. **CORRECT.** This matches. The only difference between the two products is that the FreezAll is less powerful, so that's the only reason the saleswoman has for recommending it.
You might be thinking "less power, why would I want that?". Well, maybe more powerful units break down faster and require more specialized maintenance.

Question 8

QUESTION TYPE: Necessary Assumption

CONCLUSION: It's useless to focus on the flaws of our leaders.

REASONING: We chose those leaders. We should focus on the flaws in our institutions that allowed us to choose such flawed leaders.

ANALYSIS: It can be hard to figure out what's wrong with a system unless you also look at the results it produces. So it may be hard to reform the political system unless we look at the flaws of the leaders produced by that system.

_____

A. **CORRECT.** The negation of this wrecks the argument.
Negation: Examining the flaws of an individual leader will reveal something about the flaws in the system that produced that leader.
B. Who cares? This just gets the terms under discussion backwards. We care whether discussing flaws of leaders stops us from reforming the system. This answer instead talks about whether discussion about reforming the system will affect discussion of leaders.
C. It doesn't matter whether the system is *completely* terrible.
Negation: It's possible for the system to produce a leader who isn't flawed.
D. Who cares if one person has examined the flaws of the system?
Negation: One solitary individual examined the details of the nation's institutions and procedures. But they didn't tell anyone, and then they died.
E. Public dissatisfaction is irrelevant to this question. This answer is drawing on your outside ideas that the public is dissatisfied with its leaders.

Question 9

QUESTION TYPE: Paradox

PARADOX: Calcium supplements often have lead, and lead is dangerous. We can store a small amount of lead in bones.

Doctors say that it's better to take calcium supplements with lead rather than to take no calcium supplements at all.

ANALYSIS: We know lead is bad. But that's only half the story. Calcium supplements don't only contain lead: they also have calcium.

There must be some benefit to calcium consumption that outweighs the danger from lead.

———————————

A. This makes the situation more confusing. If people are already getting trace amounts of lead from food, then extra lead from supplements is even more dangerous.

B. This is just a fact about lead. It doesn't help explain why doctors think that the lead in calcium supplements is safe.

C. Who cares? The fact that there are other causes of anemia tells us nothing about calcium supplements. We *know* that the lead in those supplements can cause anemia, that's not in question.

D. This would have been the right answer if it had said that a high calcium diet *increases* the amount of lead we can tolerate.
But this says the opposite. So taking calcium supplements makes lead even more dangerous.

E. **CORRECT.** This explains why it may be safer to take calcium supplements with lead. If we didn't have the calcium, our bones might leach even more lead.

Question 10

QUESTION TYPE: Principle Application

PRINCIPLE: Buy antique → certain about authenticity AND you like the piece

Contrapositive: Dislike piece OR not certain about authenticity → Don't buy

APPLICATION: Maude shouldn't buy the vase.

ANALYSIS: Principle Application questions are very, very routine. Here's what to do.

1. Check what the question asks you to prove. (Maude should *not* buy the vase)
2. Check what sufficient condition allows you to prove that. (Not certain about authenticity OR not liking the piece's intrinsic qualities)
3. Skim the answers to find the one that has a matching condition.

There are only two ways an answer can be correct. Anything else is a distraction. Three wrong answers try to help show Maude *should* buy the vase, which is the opposite of what we're looking for. Several answers mention investment value, which was *not* a necessary condition.

———————————

A. The fact that Maude has skill in identifying counterfeits doesn't help us prove she shouldn't buy a vase. Only *lack* of confidence proves that.

B. The principle said that value as an investment is not a decisive factor in purchasing antiques.

C. This evidence helps establish the two necessary conditions for buying a vase. We're trying to prove that Maude shouldn't buy the vase, therefore we're looking for a *lack* of a condition. You might think the documentation is fake. That's possible. But only possible. We need evidence that Maude lacks confidence before we say she shouldn't buy the vase.

D. These factors help establish Maude *should* buy the vase. We're trying to prove that she shouldn't.

E. **CORRECT.** There's no way for Maude to be certain about the authenticity of this vase. Since confidence was a necessary condition for buying, this answer lets us prove Maude shouldn't buy the vase.

Question 11

QUESTION TYPE: Most Strongly Supported

FACTS:

1. Waverly wanted to be objective.
2. Waverly wrote better about art she likes.

ANALYSIS: This is a confusing stimulus. It requires you to think in real world terms.

Bias can be subtle. If someone claims to be neutral, but they consistently write better about things they like, then that's a form of bias.

Waverly said she wanted to be neutral. Since Waverly did have a bias, we can say that it seems she failed to achieve her stated goal.

A. Waverly didn't say what all art historians should do. Instead, Waverly only described what she tried to do. Maybe Waverly thinks art historians can have opinions in other cases.
B. The critic said Waverly writes better about art she likes than about art she doesn't care about. That actually implies this answer is false: if you are indifferent to art then you won't like or dislike it.
C. Hard to say what Waverly's intention was. She may have honestly tried to write neutrally, but failed in her aim.
D. **CORRECT.** This seems probable. If you write better about art you like, then that is a form of bias.
E. This is a strong accusation. It's equally likely that Waverly wanted to be objective, but failed. Objectivity is hard.

Question 12

QUESTION TYPE: Sufficient Assumption

CONCLUSION: The Sals didn't smelt iron.

REASONING: The Sals didn't have a word for iron.

ANALYSIS: This stimulus has a lot of filler. The first sentence adds nothing; it merely tells us vaguely that there are new discoveries. Likewise, the information about bronze and copper smelting tells us nothing directly about iron.

On sufficient assumption questions you must be focussed. The author will give you a conclusion: the Sals don't smelt iron. They'll give you their evidence for that statement: The Sals had no word for iron.

There will be a gap between the conclusion and evidence. In this case, the fact that a language lacks a word for something doesn't mean the people who speak that language don't know about the thing. For instance, you know how an autumn day smells? We don't have a word for that, but we know what it is.

The right answer connects the evidence to the conclusion by saying that if a language lacks a word for a metal, then it didn't smelt that metal.

Normally you could diagram a sufficient assumption stimulus. But in this case there are just two facts, with no conditional statements to draw. The right answer connects the facts by using a conditional.

A. This gets things backwards. It says: word → smelt. We're looking for smelt → word
B. This gets the contrapositive of the right answer backwards. It says: ~~smelt~~ → ~~word~~. We're looking for ~~word~~ → ~~smelt~~
C. The question is trying to prove a point about iron. Copper and bronze are irrelevant unless they're connected to iron.
D. We're trying to *prove* that the Sals didn't smelt iron. This answer tells us what happens *if* the Sals didn't smelt iron. Such a statement can't help us prove that the Sals didn't smelt iron.
E. **CORRECT.** This connects the evidence to the conclusion. Smelt → word. Contrapositive: ~~word~~ → ~~smelt~~

Question 13

QUESTION TYPE: Identify the Conclusion

CONCLUSION: Community organizations need to convince the public that higher education is good for all of society.

REASONING: It's easier to get the public to support programs which benefit everyone, like road building.

ANALYSIS: On identify the conclusion questions, always ask yourself "why are they telling me this?". Pretend the author is a real person. In this case, the author is giving advice to community groups that want to get funding for higher education. The author is telling them *how* to make their case. The author says that community groups should argue that higher education benefits everyone.

The second sentence, that the public is receptive to widely beneficial programs, is not the conclusion. This is evidence supporting the idea that the approach in the first sentence will be effective.

The words "for example" are a structural indicator. They show that what comes after "for example" is a premise supporting the conclusion.

Note: You may think that higher education obviously benefits everybody. Why would anyone have to argue for that? The main reason you believe university benefits everyone is because you *went* to university. The American university system asserts that education benefits everyone in order to justify its existence. That claim is not a universal truth.

A. CORRECT. See the analysis above.
B. This is a premise supporting the plan of arguing that higher education benefits us all.
C. This is an example of a program that's popular because the benefits are widespread.
D. This is evidence supporting the argument that community groups should therefore argue that higher education benefits us all.
E. The author didn't say that higher education benefits us all. They said community groups should *say* that it does, in order to get funding. This is a subtle distinction, but it's important to notice these.

Question 14

QUESTION TYPE: Role in Argument

CONCLUSION: There will be a much higher risk of satellite collisions in the future.

REASONING: Once one satellite collision occurs, the accident will create lots of debris that other satellites can crash into.

ANALYSIS: This is a serious concern in the satellite realm. As far as I'm aware, we have no good way of removing debris from the atmosphere. So once a collision occurs, the extra debris will stay in orbit indefinitely.

The question is asking about the role of the statement between "but" and "after all". These words have the following structural meaning:

But: I disagree with what came before. What comes after "but" is my conclusion.

After all: The conclusion is what comes before "after all". The sentence following "after all" is evidence for the conclusion.

So the statement in question is the conclusion.

A. The statement in question *is* the conclusion. See the analysis above. It is supported, by the sentence that follows "after all".
B. The statement in question is the conclusion. See the analysis above. It is supported, by the sentence that follows "after all".
C. The statement in question is the conclusion. See the analysis above.
D. CORRECT. See the analysis above.
E. Nonsense. The statement in question is the conclusion. See the analysis above.

Question 15

QUESTION TYPE: Paradox

PARADOX: One group of chickens received salmonella treatment, the other didn't.

The group that received salmonella had less salmonella but more bacteria of other types.

ANALYSIS: Somehow, the salmonella treatment encouraged bacterial growth in the first group of chickens.

I couldn't prephrase this question. I just kept the facts above in mind, and looked for a reason why salmonella treatment could lead to more bacteria. I quickly skipped over any answer that didn't seem promising.

A. Who cares? The treatment could have taken 15 seconds or 15 days, and nothing would be different. The paradox is about what happened *after* the treatment.
B. Who cares? The stimulus just said that salmonella levels are *lower*. That's a relative term. If the starting salmonella level were 10%, then lower could be 9%. If the starting level were only 0.5%, then lower would be 0.4%. In neither case does the absolute amount of salmonella matter.
C. The stimulus is not talking about adult chickens.
D. This just makes the situation more confusing. The stimulus said that the untreated group had *fewer* non-salmonella bacteria. So why does the untreated group have more infections?
E. **CORRECT.** This explains it. Salmonella prevents some bacteria from growing. Since the treatment removed salmonella, it makes sense that other bacteria were able to grow.
The "nonvirulent" part of this answer is irrelevant. The stimulus didn't make a distinction between harmful and harmless bacteria. It just said the treated group had more bacteria, period.

Question 16

QUESTION TYPE: Flawed Reasoning

CONCLUSION: Hierarchy in lecturing is a good thing.

REASONING: All knowledge has hierarchy. We must move from simple to complex knowledge.

ANALYSIS: Hierarchy has two meanings.

1. A system of organization in which people or groups are ranked one above the other according to status or authority.
2. An arrangement or classification of things according to relative importance or inclusiveness.

The debater is using the first definition, power relations between people. The respondent incorrectly switches to the second definition, how we classify things.

Note: I took the definitions from the New Oxford American Dictionary.

A. This isn't a flaw. If an assumption in an opponents' argument is true, then you *should* agree that it's true. You can still disagree with other parts of the argument.
B. The respondent clearly said that *all* subjects must go from simple to complex. Math was just an example.
C. The argument isn't about whether lecturing on the whole has weaknesses. It's only about whether hierarchy is a strength or a weakness.
D. **CORRECT.** The key concept is the word hierarchy. The respondent uses it in a different sense. See the analysis above.
E. The respondent clearly said that *all* subjects must go from simple to complex. Math was just an example. The finer details of the conceptual structure of math don't matter.

Question 17

QUESTION TYPE: Strengthen

CONCLUSION: The ancient Chinese probably discovered Han purple by accident while making glass.

REASONING: The same ingredients and similar processes were used to make white glass and Han purple.

ANALYSIS: The argument has implied that it's *possible* that Han purple was discovered during the production of white glass. The makers of white glass were using the right ingredients, and a related process.

But the argument didn't say if Han purple was invented in a place where white glass was made! If Han purple was invented somewhere without white glass, then the conclusion is almost certainly wrong.

The right answer strengthens the argument by at least showing that white glass *could* have led to the discovery of Han purple. It restricts the production of Han purple only to an area that also produced white glass.

Note: This is a *very* hard question. The correct answer is asking you to conceptualize an alternate possibility (that Han purple was discovered in an area without white glass) and then to recognize that answer A eliminates that possibility.

There would have been a simpler way of doing that. Answer A could have said "Han purple was invented in an area where white glass was produced". But if the right answer had said that, then this question would have been to easy, wouldn't it?

A. CORRECT. This eliminates the possibility that white glass and Han purple were produced in completely separate regions.
Note: This answer would have been equally strong if it said that white glass and Han purple were each produced all over China. The main thing is that it shows the two materials were produced in the same areas, therefore accidental discovery was possible.

B. This is just an irrelevant fact about how the materials were used. We care about how they were *made*.

C. This doesn't tell us about how Han purple was invented. It tells us how many people knew how to make it *after* it was invented.

D. This shows that it would have been easy to make white glass. But that doesn't prove anything about the production of Han purple.
For instance, the material to make wheels on suitcases was easily accessible for years, but we didn't think of the idea. Upright wheeled suitcases were only invented in 1987.

E. This doesn't explain anything. Maybe white glass objects were more durable than Han purple objects. Who cares? We're only interested in what lead to the initial invention of Han purple.

Question 18

QUESTION TYPE: Flawed Reasoning

CONCLUSION: Mild sleep deprivation is probably healthy and boosts the immune system.

REASONING: People who sleep at least 8 hours a night have more diseases than those who sleep a lot less each night.

ANALYSIS: This argument confuses correlation for causation. Whenever there is a correlation, there are four possibilities:

1. Sleep does cause illness.
2. Illness causes more sleep.
3. A third factor causes both illness and sleep.
4. The correlation is a coincidence.

On a flawed reasoning question, the right answer will describe one of the other possibilities abstractly. Here, answer A describes the third possibility.

———————————

A. **CORRECT.** This is possibility three above. Perhaps, for example, a weakened immune system causes more sleep (to repair the immune system) and more infections (because the immune system is weak).
B. The argument didn't say that *only* sleep affects health. There could easily be other factors, such as genetics, exercise, diet, etc.
C. This is fancy language for taking a necessary condition to be a sufficient condition. That didn't happen here.
D. This is saying: if hammers can cause injury, then there will be a correlation between hammers and injury.
   That's flawed reasoning (hammer owners might be careful with their hammers), but it's not the flawed reasoning used in the argument.
E. This is a different flaw.
   Example of flaw: Smoking doesn't cause boils. Therefore, smoking is safe.

Question 19

QUESTION TYPE: Parallel Reasoning

CONCLUSION: Temperatures didn't go below freezing last week.

REASONING: Freezing → impatiens dead → ~~bloom~~

Contrapositive: bloom → ~~impatiens dead~~ → ~~freezing~~

The impatiens did bloom.

ANALYSIS: This argument uses a valid chain of conditional statements. We can say that if temperatures were below freezing last week, the impatiens would not have bloomed. The contrapositive above shows that since the impatiens did bloom, temperatures didn't go below freezing.

The right answer must copy these features of the argument:

1. Combines two conditional statements
2. Takes the contrapositive
3. Uses a fact to prove something with the contrapositive.

The answers are *long*. You shouldn't read them. Skim them, and look for the structural features above. Here's my quick skim

A: Has two conditionals. Contender.
B: Second sentence says "some". Eliminate.
C: Doesn't use any facts, only conditionals. First sentence is "if but only if". Eliminate.
D: Says "should". That's a moral question. Eliminate.
E: Says "should". That's a moral question. Eliminate.

Note that the LSAT strictly separates fact and morality. Answers with "should" are highly unlikely to be parallel if the stimulus is fact based.

This process left A. I then considered it more carefully, and saw it matched. Note that B-E are just soft eliminates. If A were wrong, I'd have to look at them again.

Notes on Skimming: You should practice skimming parallel reasoning answers for structure. The right question is not "how could I eliminate this" but rather "how could I eliminate this in 2-3 seconds?".

Like any other skill in life, you'll get better at this if you practice identifying the structure of the stimulus and then using that to eliminate wrong answers fast. Make a collection of long parallel reasoning questions, and redo them periodically to practice.

Note that it takes a lot of words to *explain* how I do this type of question. But it doesn't take me long to *do* this type of question, because I don't have to justify myself to anyone. A question like this one can be answered in 30 seconds.

———————————

A. CORRECT. This exactly parallels the structure:
Adaptable → Thrive → Adverse
~~Adverse~~ → ~~Thrive~~ → ~~Adaptable~~
The species has had no adverse effect, therefore it's not adaptable.

B. The first sentence is fine. The second sentence is wrong: it gives a "some" statement. This answer also makes a switch between being adaptable and actually adapting to a new environment. Those are different things, and the stimulus didn't make that distinction.

C. This is a flawed argument, and it has a different structure from the stimulus. Here's how to draw the first sentence:
Introduced AND Adapt → Adverse affect
The conclusion says that if a species doesn't adapt, then there will be no adverse effect. That's incorrectly negating a sufficient condition. Necessary conditions can happen without sufficient conditions.

D. This is a good argument, but it's just a single conditional statement, with a fact. This also includes "should" which introduces a moral element absent from the stimulus. Here's the one conditional: Adverse effect → should not introduce
The conclusion just follows the conditional by saying an adverse effect will be present, therefore the species shouldn't be introduced.

E. This answer is just a confused jumble of words. The first sentence doesn't link to anything. It tells us not to introduce species if they cause harm, but then the third sentence says that species will be introduced anyway. The second and third sentence just say, without proof, that we ought to control populations. (The benefit is that the risk of adverse impact is limited, but we don't know if there are any drawbacks to manual population control).

Question 20

QUESTION TYPE: Sufficient Assumption

CONCLUSION: Convention center → tax revenue

REASONING: Convention center → Conventions

Large conventions → visitors → tax revenues

ANALYSIS: On sufficient assumption questions, you should follow a three step process:

Identify the conclusion: CC → T
Split it apart: CC   T
Fill in the evidence: CC → C   LC → V → T

This question plays a trick. The first sentence says that a convention center will lead to more conventions. But the second sentence says that *large* conventions are what lead to visitors.

Large conventions and conventions are not the same thing; conventions can be small. This is the gap in the argument. The right answer, E, fills the gap by saying that the new conventions will be large.

———————————

A. We already knew that visitors lead to more tax revenue. This answer says that *only* visitors will lead to tax revenue. That's useless.
B. This doesn't help. The question is only about tax revenues, not money spent. We already know that visitors lead to tax revenue. It doesn't matter *how* they lead to tax revenue.
C. This answer doesn't prove anything. It says other methods of raising taxes *won't* work, but that doesn't prove that a convention center *will* work.
D. This is irrelevant. The stimulus already said visitors will increase if there are large conventions. That fact is not in doubt, and it doesn't need the support of this answer.
This doesn't help connect convention centers to large conventions or tax revenue.
E. CORRECT. This shows why you should read all the answers before committing to any. Once E points out the difference between conventions and large conventions, it may seem obvious. But you won't know that until you look at it. So don't waste 30 seconds thinking at A if you haven't looked at E yet.

Question 21

QUESTION TYPE: Argument Evaluation

CONCLUSION: Dogs don't like being treated unfairly.

REASONING: Pairs of dogs were given a command. When both dogs obeyed, only one dog was rewarded. Eventually, the dogs that didn't receive treats stopped obeying.

ANALYSIS: This question is talking about trained dogs. You surely know that dogs are often rewarded with treats or affection for obeying commands.

This argument has given a *possible* explanation for the dogs lack of obedience. Perhaps they did indeed feel they were being treated unfairly. But the argument didn't rule out a likely alternative explanation: The dogs expected treats for obedience, and stopped obeyed when there were no treats (regardless of what happened to the other dog).

———————————

A. This is irrelevant. The stimulus is only talking about situations where both dogs obey, initially.
B. CORRECT. This addresses an alternative explanation. It's quite possibly that the dogs stopped obeying simply because they weren't being rewarded. If both dogs went unrewarded and still stopped obeying, then that rules out fairness as an explanation. Both dogs received an equal, fair amount of treats: zero.
C. The *reverse* of this answer would be interesting. If some dogs who *didn't* receive treats were then given treats in later trials, that might affect the experiment. But this answer is only talking about dogs who receive treats and then later do not receive treats.
D. "*Any* cases" is quite useless. You need to take vague answers at their weakest. If *one* dog became more inclined to obey, what does that prove?
E. Who cares? The number of repetitions required doesn't change the underlying theory. It's not as if five repetitions would indicate unfairness was the cause, while ten repetitions would indicate that lack of reward was the cause.

Question 22

QUESTION TYPE: Most Strongly Supported

FACTS:

1. Satisfaction with income mostly depends on how much you make relative to your neighbors.

ANALYSIS: The stimulus does *not* say that earning more money is irrelevant to happiness. Earning more money can definitely affect happiness, but only by comparison with what your neighbors make.

Lets assume that if you make the same as your neighbors, you feel neutral about your income.

So if you earn $50,000, and your neighbors earn $50,000, you'll be very happy if you suddenly get $30,000 more per year.

Whereas if you earn $80,000, but your neighbors earn $200,000, you won't be very happy even if you suddenly get $40,000 more per year.

An *individual* will feel happier if they get richer. But an entire country or neighborhood won't feel happier if they all get richer. Happiness only depends on how rich we are *compared to others.*

A. This answer ignores neighborhoods. If high income people live with other high income people, then they won't be more satisfied than middle income people.
B. We have no idea. This would only be true if older people were more likely to have higher incomes than their neighbors.
C. This is wrong. Neighborhoods often contain people with similar incomes. In that case, satisfaction would be about the same in all neighborhoods.
D. This isn't true. The stimulus actually says that more money will make you happier, *if* it means you earn more than your neighbors.
E. **CORRECT.** Money only makes you happier if it makes you richer than your neighbors. So if everyone gets richer, then no one will be happier.

Question 23

QUESTION TYPE: Weaken

CONCLUSION: It is wrong to say that petroleum formed from lifeless deep carbon deposits.

REASONING: Petroleum has biomarkers, and biomarkers come from living things or from things that were once alive.

ANALYSIS: This argument has a missing premise. The geologist is trying to prove that the petroleum formed from living things in the past.

The presence of biomarkers isn't definitive proof, because the biomarkers could come from things that are alive *now,* or were recently. The geologist assumes, without evidence, that the biomarkers must have come from long dead life forms.

A. The author didn't say that all fossils have biomarkers. It's possible that some fossils lost their biomarkers due to the effects of time. The geologist's claim is that *if* you find a biomarker, *then* there must have been life. But something could have been alive even if we can't currently find biomarkers.
B. The author didn't say when petroleum formed. Both petroleum and living organisms might have formed long after the earth's formation. The only reference to the earth's formation is that the *carbon deposits* formed not long after the earth did. But that doesn't mean that *petroleum* formed soon after the earth did. Petroleum could have started forming later, when life existed.
C. The argument didn't say how long petroleum takes to form. Several million years could be fine.
D. **CORRECT.** If bacteria live deep in the crust, then they could live near petroleum. Perhaps the bacteria leave biomarkers in the petroleum. Therefore the biomarkers are not a sign the petroleum originally formed from life. They are merely a sign that bacteria are currently present.
E. The geologist is *defending* the dominant view that petroleum formed from fossilized plants and animals. So knowing that at least some petroleum deposits formed from plants *strengthens* the geologist's argument.

Question 24

QUESTION TYPE: Must be True

FACTS:

1. (Injury OR $500) AND Capable → Report
2. ~~Report~~ → ~~Capable~~ OR (~~Injury~~ AND ~~$500~~)
3. Ted doesn't have to report the accident.

ANALYSIS: This question uses a compound sufficient condition (Injury OR $500). I'll explain how to think about it with an example. You're trying to prove someone can buy a sandwich. You can buy a sandwich if you have: A $20 bill OR a bunch of coins OR a credit card OR a gift certificate.

It doesn't make sense to write all of those out in a conditional statement though. Really, it should be: money → can buy sandwich

That simplified statement comes from your common sense knowledge that all of the above equal money. If someone asks specifics, you know that "money" is more detailed that what you've written, but you don't need to write everything in the statement.

In the case of this question, the simplified statement would be:

Bad thing AND Capable → Report

The contrapositive is: ~~Report~~ → ~~Bad thing~~ OR ~~Capable~~

Basically, if you make a bad accident you have to report it – assuming you're capable. The only catch is that "bad accident" has two components, either of which is enough to lead to a report.

"Unless" can be a tricky word to diagram. Use your common sense to think about what the word means. Making up examples to test the word is helpful.

For instance, go to work when you're healthy unless there is a thunderstorm is: Healthy AND ~~thunderstorm~~ → go to work

You negate whatever is after unless and make it a sufficient condition.

Since Ted doesn't have to report the accident, we can say that either he's not capable, or the accident wasn't bad. Which in this case means both conditions for bad are out: no injury, and less than $500.

A. If Ted is incapable of reporting, then we have no condition that can force him to report. So we have no idea how bad the damage is.

B. **CORRECT.** This is true. Normally, you have to report over $500 if you're the driver. Ted doesn't have to report, so he must not be capable. That's the only exception to the rule.

C. The stimulus only talks about the driver's responsibility to report. Perhaps no other person ever has legal responsibility to report.

D. There may be other reasons Ted is incapable of reporting. Perhaps he is far from any city, and he has no phone.

E. This may not be true. It's possible that someone was injured, but Ted is incapable of reporting. In that case, Ted doesn't have to report.

Question 25

QUESTION TYPE: Flawed Parallel Reasoning

CONCLUSION: Many people must be immune to staphylococcus.

REASONING: Many people are exposed to staphylococcus and don't develop symptoms. Immunity is one possible cause for not developing symptoms.

ANALYSIS: This argument mistakes a sufficient condition for a necessary condition. It gives us this statement:

Immunity to staphylococcus → ~~symptoms~~

The argument then shows that some people met the necessary condition: they were exposed and had no symptoms.

The argument incorrectly went backwards. You can't go backwards with conditionals. We can't conclude that some who were exposed had immunity. (Maybe they had good immune systems in general, but with no specific immunity to staphylococcus).

To parallel the argument, look for these elements:

1. A conditional statement.
2. A statement that says some cases met the necessary condition.
3. A conclusion that goes backwards and incorrectly concludes the sufficient condition.

A. This isn't the same. This argument has a conditional statement, and also a "some" statement that adds a new term. That is enough to make this the wrong answer.
The "some" statement in this argument does allow a valid deduction, though the argument doesn't make it.
Moral → Just
Serve interest SOME ~~Just~~ → ~~Moral~~
Deduction: Serve interest SOME ~~Moral~~
The conclusion of this argument is wrong. It's an incorrect negation of the valid "some" statement above. The conclusion was: ~~Serve Interest~~ SOME Moral

B. There are no "some" statements given in this answer, just two conditionals. And the conclusion says "probably", which is structurally different from the absolute conclusion in the stimulus.
Note that the conclusion is wrong: it incorrectly assumes that anyone who tries to persuade is probably an advertiser. (This isn't *quite* an incorrect negation, because of the "probably)
Advertiser → Persuade
Fiction → ~~Advertiser~~
Conclusion: Fiction (probably)→ ~~Persuade~~

C. This argument ignores a possibility. It's possible Isabel took the medication, and it alleviated her symptoms even though she's still quite sick. You can be somewhat *better,* even though your situation is still *bad*. You'd need to prove that there was no cure AND no alleviation before you said that Isabel didn't take the medicine.
So, the author misunderstands how compound necessary conditions work. That doesn't match the reversal error in the stimulus.
Diagram: Medicine → Cure or Alleviate

D. **CORRECT.** This exactly matches the incorrect reversal.
Taxation → ~~expansion~~
The author states the necessary condition occurred, and then incorrectly goes backward to say that there must have been taxation.

E. This argument is just wrong. There are plenty of reasons doctors might wash their hands less than other health professionals.
1. Doctors are lazy and careless, OR
2. Doctors are in fewer situations where hand-washing is required.
Who knows? In any case, this argument is completely different from the incorrect reversal in the stimulus.

Section II – Logic Games
Game 1 – Band Concert
Questions 1–5

Setup

This is a pure sequencing game. This type of game has been changing on modern LSATs.

If you look at older LSATs, say, earlier than PT 40, you'll see that sequencing games were very, very, standardized. Do one and you could do all of them easily.

This worked in the early days, because not that many people prepped for the LSAT. Standard sequencing games were hard if you had never seen them before.

But since they were the most learnable logic game, students who prepped started doing really, really well on sequencing games. It was an unfair advantage.

So the LSAC began throwing twists into sequencing games. The underlying logic was the same, but the games became more complex.

This game continues that trend. It introduces dual scenarios into a sequencing game, which I've never seen before. Study this game well, and repeat it a few times. I expect this game will become one of the standard types on future sequencing games.

We'll start with the basic setup. Here's the diagram, plus the 1st rule (the guitarist doesn't perform fourth):

① $\underline{\quad}$ $\underline{\quad}$ $\underline{\quad}$ $\underline{\quad}$ $\underline{\quad}$ $\underline{\quad}$
    1 2 3 4 5 6
             G̸

Next, rule 2 says that the percussionist is before the keyboard player:

P—K

The third rule also mentions the keyboard player, so it can be combined with the first rule. It's very useful to combine sequencing rules:

P—K—G
    /
V

This digram lets us see, for example, that the percussionist performs before the guitarist.

The final rule is the most complicated rule of the game. First, you must think about the full implications of the rule. It says that the saxophonist is after the trumpeter, or the percussionist, *but not both*.

The saxophonist can only be before *one of the* trumpeter or the percussionist. So if the saxophonist is after the percussionist, then the saxophonist is *before* the trumpeter. And vice versa:

P—S—T
    or
T—S—P

The reverse is also possible. Effectively, the saxophonist has to be between the percussionist and the trumpeter.

You could stop here, but there's more to deduce. For instance, look what happens if you combine T−S−P with rules 2 and 3:

$$T-S-P\overset{K-G}{\underset{V}{}}$$

If T−S−P are in that order, we know almost everything. The only uncertainty is where V goes. It could go anywhere earlier than K, including first.

What about P−S−T? We can draw a combined diagram there as well:

$$P-S-T\overset{K-G}{\underset{V}{}}$$

We're still not done. You always must consider restricted variables. G is very restricted. Let's see what we know about G:

- G can't be fourth.
- G has to be after P, K and V

We can combine those to say that G can't be in the first four spaces. So P, K, V and at least one other band member must be before G. In the diagram above, that means S must be before G:

$$P-S-T\\ \qquad K-G\\ V$$

So we have two scenarios. They depend on whether the order is P−S−T or T−S−P:

Scenario 1 (T−S−P)

$$T-S-P\overset{K-G}{\underset{V}{}}$$

Scenario 2 (P−S−T)

$$P-S-T\\ \qquad K-G\\ V$$

These diagrams make solving the game lightning fast. If a question asks what "could be true", you can just check if an answer is possible in either diagram.

Note that you should draw both of these diagrams on the *second* page, under the questions. That way, it's faster to refer to the diagrams when solving questions.

Main Diagram

These are the combined diagrams. They contain every rule. The diagrams will be confusing if you don't know how to build them. Look back to the setup section to see how to create these diagrams.

Scenario 1 (T−S−P)

$$T-S-P\overset{K-G}{\underset{V}{}}$$

Scenario 2 (P−S−T)

$$P-S-T\\ \qquad K-G\\ V$$

Question 1

For acceptable order questions, go through the rules and use them to eliminate answers one by one.

Note that I use the rules themselves. I don't use my diagrams for these questions. Reading the rules again for this question will help you memorize the rules, and it's also more efficient.

Rule 1 eliminates **A.** The guitarist can't be fourth.

Rule 2 eliminates **D** and **E.** The percussionist has to be before the keyboard player.

Rule 3 eliminates no answers.

Rule 4 eliminates **B.** The saxophonist has to be between the trumpeter and the percussionist.

C is **CORRECT.** It violates no rules.

Question 2

In the setup, I showed how all of the rules could be reduced to two diagrams. The diagrams depended on whether the order from the fourth rule was P–S–T or T–S–P.

This question tells us that the percussionist is before the saxophonist, so the order is P–S–T. This diagram is the one that applies:

```
P—S—T
 \   \
  >K—G
 /
V
```

You can use the diagram to eliminate answers one by one. You're looking for something that *must* be true in the diagram, so your goal should be to prove that the wrong answers could be false.

A doesn't have to be true. The violinist could be before the percussionist. Since neither the violinist nor the percussionist have anyone before them on the diagram, either could go first.

B doesn't have to be true. The percussionist could be before everyone if we place the violinist after the percussionist.

C doesn't have to be true. The diagram only places the violinist before the keyboard player. There's no direct link between these and the saxophonist.

D is **CORRECT.** You can see this by following the lines on the diagram. P is before G.

E doesn't have to be true. There are no lines linking the keyboard player and the saxophone player, so either of them could go before the other.

Question 3

This is a "must be false EXCEPT" question. That means the right answer is something that could be true.

Go one by one through the answers and scan both diagrams from the setup. If an answer is possible in either scenario, it's the right answer. Here are the diagrams again:

Scenario 1 (T–S–P)

```
T—S—P—K—G
         /
        V
```

Scenario 2 (P–S–T)

```
P—S—T
 \   \
  >K—G
 /
V
```

A must be false. In both diagrams, the keyboardist is after some other band member.

B must be false. In both diagrams, the guitarist is after at least the percussionist, the keyboardist and the saxophonist.

C must be false. In both diagrams the saxophonist is before the guitarist.

D must be false. In both diagrams the percussionist is before the guitarist.

E is **CORRECT.** In the P–S–T diagram, the keyboardist could be before the saxophonist. That's because they have no lines directly connecting them: either could go first. For example, this order obeys the rules:

P	V	K	S	G	T
1	2	3	4	5	6
			Ⱦ		

28

Question 4

This is a CANNOT be true question. For this question, you should think about who is restricted. The question asks who can't go third, so you should look for a variable that has other variables in front of it.

G is restricted thanks to the second and the third rules. P, K and V all must go in front of G:

P—K—G
V

So the guitarist always has at least three other players in front. **A** is **CORRECT.**

Question 5

This question says the violinist performs the fourth solo. We also know from the rules that the violinist has to be before the keyboardist and the guitarist. So we get this order:

$$\frac{}{1} \quad \frac{}{2} \quad \frac{}{3} \quad \frac{V}{4} \quad \frac{K}{5} \quad \frac{G}{6}$$
G

The only players left are P, S and T. We know from rule four that those must be in one of two orders:

- P–S–T
- T–S–P

So we get these two diagrams:

$$\frac{P}{1} \quad \frac{S}{2} \quad \frac{T}{3} \quad \frac{V}{4} \quad \frac{K}{5} \quad \frac{G}{6}$$
G

$$\frac{T}{1} \quad \frac{S}{2} \quad \frac{P}{3} \quad \frac{V}{4} \quad \frac{K}{5} \quad \frac{G}{6}$$
G

The question is asking for "what must be true EXCEPT". That means the right answer is something that could be false. Since only P, S and T can be switched, the answer will surely use those variables.

E is **CORRECT.** The trumpeter doesn't have to be before the saxophonist. We can see this in the first diagram above.

Game 2 – Art Historians
Questions 6–10

Setup

This is an unusual linear game. It's unusual because it has two different groups, and some of the ordering rules cross over between groups. Here's how to set up the main diagram:

```
s ___  ___  ___  ___

h ___  ___  ___  ___
    1    2    3    4
```

The first rule says that O and W are before L. So far, that's standard:

```
O
 >L
W
```

It's the second rule that's confusing. This rule says that F is before O:

```
F—O
```

Why is this confusing? Because F is a lecture, and O, W, L are subjects. So F and W could actually be in the same spot, like this:

```
s  S   W   O   L
   __  __  __  __

h  __  F   __  __
    1   2   3   4
```

As long as you remember that F and W can go together, this game is easy. Otherwise, it's hard, and it's best to draw the O, W, L and F, O rules separately, like this. Then you can check them separately to rule out violations:

```
O
 >L
W

F—O
```

If you can handle the ambiguity, it's cleaner to combine the rules. Just remember that F and W are different types of variables and could go together:

```
F—O
    >L
   W
```

The final rule is about speakers. H is in front of G and J:

```
    G
H<
    J
```

Finally, the sculptures lecture is random, it has no rules:

There are a couple of up front deductions. We can say which lecturers go where:

- F has at least two people after it: those that lecture on O and L
- H has at least two people after it: G and J

This means that both F and H can go second at latest. That's the only way to leave two spaces after them:

```
s ___  ___  ___  ___

h  F    H   ___  ___
   1    2    3    4
    \___/
```

The line under F and H means that the two variables are reversible.

Since F and H go first and second, G and J go must go third and fourth:

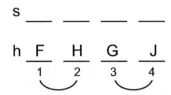

Again, the lines underneath the letters mean they're interchangeable.

This deduction about FH and GJ makes it much faster to draw diagrams. You should always take some time to examine your setup for small deductions like this before moving on. This is the key to going fast on logic games.

Main Diagram

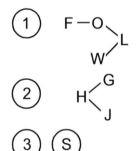

Remember, F is a lecturer, and O, W and L are subjects. So F could be in the same place as W.

In the diagram above, FH must go first and second in either order. GJ must go third and fourth in either order. I explain this deduction in the setup. But briefly, it's because both F and H each have at least two variables after them.

Question 6

For acceptable order questions, go through the rules and use them to eliminate answers one by one.

Note that I use the rules themselves. I don't use my diagrams for these questions. Reading the rules again for this question will help you memorize the rules, and it's also more efficient.

Rule 1 eliminates **A.** Oil and watercolors are supposed to be before lithographs.

Rule 2 eliminates **D.** Farley is supposed to lecture before oil paintings.

Rule 3 eliminates **C.** Holden is supposed to be before Garcia.

Rule 4 eliminates **B.** Holden is supposed to be before Jiang.

E is **CORRECT.** It violates no rules.

Question 7

Open ended must be true questions are tricky. Often, they depend on some deduction from the setup. But this game offers no useful setup deductions.

So instead, you should read through each answer and ask: are the variables in this answer restricted, or flexible?

If a variable is flexible, then it's highly unlikely to be a "must be true" answer, because flexible variables can go in many places.

For instance, **A** mentioned sculptures. But there are *no* rules for sculptures. So **A** is highly unlikely to be correct. This diagram disproves it:

s <u>S</u>   <u>W</u>   <u>O</u>   <u>L</u>

h <u>H</u>   <u>F</u>   <u>G</u>   <u>J</u>
   1   2   3   4

(Under time pressure, you wouldn't draw that diagram to disprove A. Once you see that S is random, skip the answer to look for a better candidate).

Interchangeable variables are also good candidates for elimination. For instance, G and J are exactly the same. Their only rule is that they're after H, so they're interchangeable with each other.

That means **C** and **D** are both wrong. Two answers can't be right, and there's no difference between G and J.

B is a likely candidate, because it deals with two restricted variables. Both H and L have a lot of restrictions. H must be before two variables, and L is after two variables. That means H can go second at latest, and L can go third at earliest. Here's an example:

s <u>W</u>   <u>O</u>   <u>L</u>   <u>S</u>

h <u>F</u>   <u>H</u>   <u>J</u>   <u>G</u>
   1   2   3   4

So **B** is **CORRECT,** since there's no way to avoid putting H before L.

I found **E** difficult to disprove. But since I already was 100% certain **B** was right, it wasn't essential to be completely sure **E** was wrong. Especially since G is an interchangeable variable, and that makes **E** unlikely to be right.

That said, here's a diagram to disprove **E:**

s <u>S</u>   <u>O</u>   <u>W</u>   <u>L</u>

h <u>F</u>   <u>H</u>   <u>G</u>   <u>J</u>
   1   2   3   4

I'll explain how to make a diagram like this quickly. **E** says that W has to be before G. So to prove **E** wrong, we need to see if we can put W later or at the same place as G.

To see if that's possible, concentrate on W and G separately. Put W as late as possible, and put G as early as possible. Don't try to think about it in your head: draw it. If you obey the rules, you'll get the right drawing. That's what I did above, the diagram clearly shows that **E** doesn't have to be true.

Question 8

This question places the watercolors lecture third. Whenever a question gives you a new rule, you should draw it, then ask what deductions you can make using the existing rules.

Here's W third:

```
s  __  __  W   __

h  __  __  __  __
   1   2   3   4
```

Then, see how this new rule affects the existing rules. W is mentioned in this diagram:

```
F —O
     \
      >L
   W /
```

So we need to put L after W. And we also have to put F before O. The only way to do that is like this:

```
s  __  O   W   L

h  F   __  __  __
   1   2   3   4
```

Now we can fill in the remaining variables. S is the only subject left, and it goes first.

The lecturers are H, G and J. The rules say to put H before G and J:

```
s  S   O   W   L

h  F   H   G   J
   1   2   3   4
          \___/
```

G and J are interchangeable. Since this is a "could be true" question, the right answer will almost certainly involve one of them. Note that the line under G and J indicates they're reversible.

E is CORRECT. The diagram above shows that it's possible for J to lecture on lithographs.

Question 9

This is a general cannot be true question. There's no way to answer it in advance. Instead, you should look through the answers to see which of them involve variables that have a lot of restrictions.

A is CORRECT. This diagram from the rules shows that F has to go *before* L:

```
F —O
     \
      >L
   W /
```

B, C and **E** are wrong because they involve interchangeable variables (G and J). Since there's no difference between G and J, they're highly unlikely to be the right answer on a cannot be true question.

(Technically, it would be possible for an interchangeable variable to be part of the right answer on a must be true/false question, but I've never seen it happen. They're too flexible.)

This diagram proves that **D** is wrong:

```
s  S   O   W   L

h  F   H   G   J
   1   2   3   4
          \___/
```

Question 10

In the setup, I explained that G and J must go third and fourth. That's because both F and H need at least two lecturers after them.

So if G is with S, they must both go third or both go fourth. We can use this to make two scenarios. S and G go third, and J goes fourth, and then vice versa:

Scenario 1

```
s  __  __   S   __

h  __  __   G   J
   1   2    3   4
```

Scenario 2

```
s  __  __  __   S

h  __  __   J   G
   1   2    3   4
```

Next, we can fill in the existing rules. F–O–L take up three spaces, so there's only one way to place them::

Scenario 1

```
s  __   O   S   L

h   F  __   G   J
    1   2   3   4
```

Scenario 2

```
s  __   O   L   S

h   F  __   J   G
    1   2   3   4
```

Then, only W and H are left to place, in the only open spaces.

Scenario 1

```
s  W   O   S   L

h  F   H   G   J
   1   2   3   4
```

Scenario 2

```
s  W   O   L   S

h  F   H   J   G
   1   2   3   4
```

A is CORRECT. In the second diagram, L can be third.

None of the other answers are possible in either diagram.

34

Game 3 – Woven Rugs
Questions 11–16

Setup

This is a tricky game to *explain*. It's not necessarily a hard game to *do*. That's because this game depends on your ability to see how the rules combine. There are almost no upfront deductions, and not even a good general template you can make. So my explanations for this are limited because I can't go inside your mind to show you how to see the game.

This game is a test of your visualization abilities. I am firmly convinced that *how* you lay diagrams out on your page significantly affects how well and fast you can do games. I do two things:

- My main diagram is on the *second* page, just under the questions.
- I make new diagrams for each question that requires it.

This significantly reduces eye tracking time. If your diagram is right beside answers, there is no delay between seeing the diagram and judging whether an answer is possible.

Having the main diagram on the second page also helps you reference it faster. I don't draw anything else in the main diagram area. Having a page free of clutter reduces how hard your brain has to work at understanding the diagram.

There's one more trick: make things explicit.

For instance, suppose a question places O and P. It's helpful to then draw a list of who's left beside the diagram: F, W, T, Y.

Drawing F, W, T, Y seems obvious, and therefore useless. But having the remaining variables visible lets you mentally move them onto the diagram. This removes the need to draw multiple diagrams to test the slight changes.

Ok, enough preamble. Lets see how to draw these rules. I'll note that there are rules in the setup paragraph too:

- Exactly 5/6 rug colors are used.
- Rug colors aren't repeated.

The first one is most important. If one color is out, that means *all the other colors are in*.

Note also that no rug can have more than three colors. The possible color distributions among rugs are as follows:

- 3-1-1
- 2-2-1

Those are the only ways to have three rugs that have a total of five colors.

Ok, the first rule: if white is used, then two other colors are used.

$$\underline{W} \quad \underline{} \quad \underline{} \mid$$

Note that this forces the game into a 3-1-1 color distribution.

Next, if orange is in, then it goes with peach. This leads to a deduction I'll discuss later:

$$O \rightarrow OP$$

Rules 3, 4 and 5 say who can't go together:

$$\cancel{FT} \quad \cancel{PT} \quad \cancel{PY}$$

This last rule isn't worth completely memorizing. Instead, have a clear drawing that you can reference in a split-second. Though I did remember that both forest and turquoise were mentioned in two of the exclusion rules.

I mentioned there was a deduction. Deductions come from looking at all of the rules and thinking about how they interact. Deductions also come from past experience on other games. If you know past games well enough, you'll see similar deductions on new games.

We need five colors. If any one color is out, then all the others are in.

This has a big effect on purple. If orange is out, then purple is in (because *all* other colors are in). And if orange is in, then purple is in (rule 2).

So either way, purple is *always* in. This solves question 12 instantly. Surprisingly, this deduction wasn't useful on any of the other questions.

Main Diagram

1 ___

2 ___

3 ___

Rules

① W ___ ___ |

② O → OP

③ ҒT P̶T P̶Y̶

Question 11

For acceptable order questions, go through the rules and use them to eliminate answers one by one.

Note that I use the rules themselves. I don't use my diagrams for these questions. Rereading the rules helps you to memorize them, and it's also more efficient.

Rule 1 eliminates **E.** White must go with two other colors.

Rule 2 eliminates **C.** Olive must go with purple.

Rule 3 eliminates **D.** Forest and turquoise can't go together.

Rule 5 eliminates **B.** Peach and yellow can't go together.

A is **CORRECT.** It violates no rules.

Question 12

In the setup, I described the following deduction: P has to be in.

Why? We need five colors. If any one color is out, then all the others are in.

This has a big effect on purple. If orange is out, then purple is in (because *all* other colors are in). And if orange is in, then purple is in (rule 2).

So **C** is **CORRECT.** Peach has to be used.

All of the other answers don't have to be true. This scenario disproves **A, B** and **E:**

1 W   O   P

2 F

3 T

This scenario disproves **D:**

1 W   O   P

2 F

3 Y

Remember, if something isn't forbidden, it's allowed. You should not agonize over whether a hypothetical scenario "works". If it breaks no rules, it's allowed.

So it should not take you much time to draw a scenario that doesn't violate rules, in order to disprove a specific answer. Because *anything* works if it doesn't break a rule.

Question 13

This question uses a step by step pattern of deductions to determine almost everything. I'll show you the eight steps. This is how the LSAT wants you to think.

Step 1: The question says P is alone. So draw that:

1 ___

2 ___

3 P |

Step 2: Check rules. Notice rule 2 means O is out, since P is alone.

Step 3: Notice that since one variable is out, the others are all in. (Because 5/6 colors are in)

Step 4: Notice this means white is in. Draw it:

1 W ___ ___ |

2 ___ |

3 P |

Step 5: List the remaining variables: F, T, Y

Step 6: Notice that the exclusion rules mean that F and T don't go together.

Step 7: Notice that there are only two groups left. See that this means that F and T are in separate groups:

1 W   F/T   ___ |

2 T/F |

3 P |

Step 8: Notice that only one space is left for yellow:

```
1 W  F/T  Y |
2 T/F|
3 P
```

These steps take a lot of text to describe. But if you know the rules, you can move through them in 10-15 seconds. Practice by redoing this game and seeing how fast you can do this question by following the steps.

E is **CORRECT.** White and yellow must go together in a rug.

Question 14

A solid rug is a rug with only a single color. So if there are two solid rugs, things look like this:

```
1 ___  ___  ___ |
2 ___ |
3 ___ |
```

The questions who *can't* be the two solid rugs. An open ended question like this can paralyze you. How can you get past paralysis?

You should *not* sit there, stare at the answers, and try to think of which one is impossible. At least, don't spend more than five seconds doing this. If the answer isn't immediately obvious, you will easily waste 30+ seconds if you just stare at the answers. Questions like this aren't answered in your head. Instead, you can prove answers wrong faster by drawing.

Just draw a working diagram to show the first answer is possible, like this:

```
1 W  Y  T |
2 F |
3 P |
```

That diagram proves **A** is wrong. I then used the diagram to disprove the other answers. I looked at the diagram and I swapped around variables in my head. I believe almost anyone can do this, if they know the rules and have a feel for the game.

It's hard to visualize an *entire* diagram from scratch (I can't do it easily). But it's not hard to move around a couple pieces from a diagram.

For instance, to disprove B, I made the two solo rugs F and Y. That's close to what I already drew; I just swapped P and Y. So my top diagram was W, P, T instead of W, Y and T.

But then I saw the top group couldn't be WPT, because PT couldn't go together. So I visualized the top group as W, O, P instead:

```
1 W   O   P |
2 F |
3 Y |
```

That diagram is valid. Hopefully the process I used to arrive at it made sense. I want to show you *how* I solve the question, not just make a diagram that explains why **B** is wrong.

You might feel nervous about trying to visualize new diagrams. Is what you've made an ok diagram? Most likely, Yes! This game only has three main rules:

- W goes with two other colors
- If O is in, P is in
- These don't go together: ~~FT~~, ~~PT~~, ~~FY~~

As long as you don't violate one of those rules, then *any diagram you draw is valid*. Realize this, and you'll have mastered one of the keys to logic games.

A slight switch from the diagram from **A** proves that **C** is wrong. I just looked at that diagram and swapped F and T:

```
1 W   Y   F |
2 T |
3 P |
```

For **E**, I took the diagram from A and swapped YT with FP:

```
1 W   T   P |
2 Y |
3 F |
```

Finally, **D** is **CORRECT.** Here's why it's impossible. If P and Y are alone, then the remaining options are W, O, F and T.

But, O isn't an option, because O must go with P. So we would have to place W, F and T in a rug. This doesn't work, because rule three says that F and T can't go together.

I encourage you to review this question, and draw my diagram for A on a sheet of paper:

```
1 W   O   P |
2 F |
3 Y |
```

Then mentally move around variables, to practice disproving the other answers in your head, using the aid of a working diagram. Follow the steps I list for each answer.

This method is hard to explain on paper, but once it clicks, you'll see that it's *very* effective.

Question 15

This question says that F and P are used together in a rug. That leaves W, T, O and Y left to place.

The first question is whether the color distribution is 3-1-1 or 2-2-1. (F and P would be together in one of the multi-color rugs)

2-2-1 is pretty hard to do. Of the four remaining variables, only TY could go together. So we could have FP, TY, but....neither W nor O can go alone (rules 1 and 2).

So a 2-2-1 distribution is impossible on this question. Instead, we need a 3-1-1 distribution.

So who can go with F and P? That depends on whether O is in. If O is in, O must go with FP:

1 <u>F</u>　<u>P</u>　<u>O</u>|
2 <u>　</u>|
3 <u>　</u>|

That means W *isn't* in, since W must be in a group of three. So T and Y form the solid rugs:

1 <u>F</u>　<u>P</u>　<u>O</u>|
2 <u>T</u>|
3 <u>Y</u>|

What if O isn't in? Then *all* other rugs must be in, so W is included and is in the group of three with FP:

1 <u>F</u>　<u>P</u>　<u>W</u>|
2 <u>T</u>|
3 <u>Y</u>|

T and Y form the solid rugs, since they're the only ones left.

B is CORRECT. It's possible in the first diagram. None of the other answers are possible in either diagram.

Question 16

I had no real method on this question. I simply drew the setup and looked at the first answer. It was correct.

This happens more often than you'd think. The LSAT wants you to panic. If you don't see any deductions, sometimes there are none, and it's time to move to the answers.

But set things up well first. Here's what I drew:

W,O,P,F,T

1 <u>Y</u>|
2 <u>　</u>
3 <u>　</u>

I drew all the remaining variables on top. This lets me quickly see how they interact.

A is CORRECT. It can't be true that there's only one solid color rug. If there's only one solid color rug, then the distribution is 2-2-1.

If the distribution is 2-1-1, then W is out (rule 1). That leave O, P, F and T. OP have to go together (rule 2).

That leaves F and T. And rule 3 says they can't go together in the remaining rug.

There's no need to disprove the other answers. Nonetheless, this diagram disproves **B, C** and **E**:

1 <u>Y</u>|
2 <u>W</u>　<u>O</u>　<u>P</u>|
3 <u>F</u>|

This diagram disproves **D**:

1 <u>Y</u>|
2 <u>F</u>　<u>O</u>　<u>P</u>|
3 <u>T</u>|

Game 4 – Graduation Photography
Questions 17–23

Setup

This game can be divided into two scenarios that greatly simplify the game. This is a common trend on modern logic games, so be sure you understand this setup.

I recommend drawing the diagrams on a sheet of paper yourself in order to follow along. Ideally, print a fresh copy of the game to use.

In this game, there are two groups: Silva and Thorne. Each group needs at least two photographers:

S __ __

T __ __

FH go together:

Technically this is a linear diagram, but it works just as well for grouping. Using the same symbols in both cases makes for simpler diagrams.

Next, L and M can't go together:

Next, if G is in S, then L is in T:

$$G_S \rightarrow L_T$$

$$\cancel{L}_T \rightarrow \cancel{G}_S$$

I drew the diagram and its contrapositive in this explanation. On my own sheet, I didn't draw the contrapositive because I can do it in my head. When you are still learning contrapositives, draw them, but aim to be able to instantly see them in your head.

The next rule is complicated. It says that if K *isn't* assigned to T, then H and M must both go in T.

We could leave it at that, but both H and M were mentioned in other rules. F is with H, and L can't go with M. So the full effect of the rule is this:

$$\cancel{K}_T \rightarrow FH_T \text{ and } M_T \rightarrow \cancel{L}_T$$

There's still more. If something complicated happens when a rule occurs, follow the idea as far as it goes. It's best to draw the scenario.

Lets do that. If K isn't with T, then F, H and M are there:

S __ __

$\cancel{K}$T F̲ H̲ M̲

We also know that L isn't with T, because M is there (rule 2). This affects rule 3: G can't go with S.

$\cancel{G}$ S __ __

$\cancel{L}$ $\cancel{K}$T F̲ H̲ M̲

There's till more. S needs at least two photographers. FHM are already at T. G can't go to S. So only L and K are left, and they *must* go to S:

$$G$$

$\cancel{G}$ S L̲ K̲|

$\cancel{L}$ $\cancel{K}$T F̲ H̲ M̲

Only G is left uncertain. They could go to T, or they could not be assigned. (Not all photographers have to go somewhere).

So if K isn't assigned to T, then we know almost *everything*. The scenario above is the only possible scenario.

Therefore, in all other scenarios, K *is* assigned to T:

S __ __

T _K_ __

Drawing K there may not seem like a major deduction, but this has two *big* effects.

- We no longer have to remember the fourth rule. This significantly reduces the difficulty of working with the remaining rules.
- The deduction about K solves questions 18 completely, and largely solves 19, 20, and 21.

There are big payoffs for seeing if a game can be split into two scenarios.

Main Diagram

There are two scenarios. Either K is with T:

S __ __

T _K_ __

Or K is not with T, and this happens:

```
                    G
   ☒ S  L   K |
 ↯ ✗T  F   H   M
```

See the setup for how to find the two scenarios. Here are the rules. Note that I haven't drawn the fourth rule, since the two scenarios above account for that rule.

①

②

③ $G_S \rightarrow L_T$

   $K_T \rightarrow \not{G}_S$

Question 17

For acceptable order questions, go through the rules and use them to eliminate answers one by one.

Note that I use the rules themselves. I don't use my diagrams for these questions. This helps you memorize the rules, and it's also more efficient.

Rule 1 eliminates **B.** F and H must be assigned somewhere, together.

Rule 2 eliminates **C.** L and M can't go together.

Rule 3 eliminates **A.** If G is assigned to S, then L must be assigned to T.

Rule 4 eliminates **D.** K isn't assigned to T, so H and M need to be assigned to T.

E is **CORRECT.** It violates no rules.

Question 18

This question asks what has to be true if H and L are assigned to the same ceremony. The fourth rule completely solves this. In the setup, we saw that if K is *not* assigned to T, then this happens:

```
              G
   Ŝ S L  K |
   Ŀ K̸ T  F  H  M
```

In that scenario, H and L are *not* together. So that's not the right scenario for this question. Of course, the only alternative scenario is to put K in T:

```
S __ __
T K __
```

That solves the question. **D is CORRECT.** K must be assigned to T.

Question 19

This question is similar to the elimination questions that are usually the first questions on games. You can use the rules to eliminate answers.

Note that the answers are listing people assigned to Silva.

Rule 1 eliminates **D**. H and F must go together.

Rule 4 eliminates **A**. If K is assigned to S, then they aren't at T. So H should have been assigned to T.

Rule 4 also eliminates **C**, in combination with rules 2 and 3. Actually, we saw this in the setup. If K isn't assigned to T, then G can't be assigned to S. Because that would force both M and L to be assigned to T, which violates rule 2.

Rule 4 also eliminates **E**. If K is assigned to S, then M must be assigned to T, not S.

B is CORRECT. This scenario matches **B** and violates no rules:

```
S F  G  H
T K  L
```

Question 20

In the setup, we saw that the fourth rule created two scenarios. This is what happens if K is *not* assigned to T:

```
                        G
   S̸ S L̲ K̲|
   L̸ K̸ T F̲ H̲ M̲
```

To make another scenario, the only other possibility is to assign K to T:

```
   S __ __

   T K̲ __
```

So K must always be in one of the groups. This eliminates **A, D** and **E,** as those answer don't include K.

Both **C** and **D** include FH, as they must, thanks to rule 1. The only difference between the two answers is whether L needs to be included.

This scenario proves that L doesn't need to be included:

```
   S F̲ H̲
   T K̲ G̲
```

Therefore, **B** is **CORRECT.** Only F, H and K need to be included.

Question 21

In the setup, I described how the fourth rule divides the game into two scenarios. Those scenarios make it easier to solve this question, because this question only includes four photographers.

The first scenario showed what happens if K is *not* assigned to T. That scenario has five people, so it doesn't work for this question:

```
                        G
   S̸ S L̲ K̲|
   L̸ K̸ T F̲ H̲ M̲
```

So instead we must use the alternate scenario where K *is* assigned to T:

```
   S __ __|
   T K̲ __|
```

The vertical lines indicate that both groups are full, because this question says only four photographers are included. Each group must have two of the photographers, because the opening paragraph of the setup says so.

Next, think about the rules. The first rule says that FH must be assigned to a group. Only S has two open spaces:

```
   S F̲ H̲|
   T K̲ __|
```

This solves the question. F must be assigned to S, and therefore **A** is **CORRECT.**

Question 22

This question asks which list of photographers assigned to Thorne *cannot* work.

First, remember that if a situation isn't forbidden, it's allowed. As long as a scenario doesn't violate any rules, it's fine! So you have considerable liberty in making scenarios to test whether answers are possible.

You should also use past scenarios to speed things up. For instance, this scenario from the setup shows that **A** is possible:

$$
\begin{array}{c}
 \quad\quad\quad\quad G \\
\cancel{G}\ \text{S}\ \underline{\text{L}}\ \ \underline{\text{K}}\,| \\
\cancel{L}\,\cancel{K}\ \text{T}\ \underline{\text{F}}\ \ \underline{\text{H}}\ \ \underline{\text{M}}
\end{array}
$$

G was the only remaining option in the above scenario, and it's definitely possible to place G in T.

A was the only answer without K in T. That simplifies the remaining scenarios. As long as K is in T, the game is open ended. You just have to obey these three rules:

- FH together, somewhere.
- LM apart.
- If G is in S, L is in T.

B is **CORRECT.** To see why, consider who is in S. **B** places four photographers in T. Each group needs two photographers, so that means only G and L are left to place in S. But rule 3 says that if G is in S, then L is in T.

This scenario proves that **C** is possible:

$$
\begin{array}{cccc}
\text{S} & \underline{\text{F}} & \underline{\text{H}} & \\
\text{T} & \underline{\text{G}} & \underline{\text{K}} & \underline{\text{L}}
\end{array}
$$

This scenario proves that **D** is possible:

$$
\begin{array}{cccc}
\text{S} & \underline{\text{F}} & \underline{\text{H}} & \\
\text{T} & \underline{\text{G}} & \underline{\text{K}} & \underline{\text{M}}
\end{array}
$$

This scenario proves that **E** is possible:

$$
\begin{array}{ccc}
\text{S} & \underline{\text{F}} & \underline{\text{H}} \\
\text{T} & \underline{\text{K}} & \underline{\text{M}}
\end{array}
$$

C, **D** and **E** are basically the same. The placements in T violates no rules, and you can (and must) legally place FH in S.

Question 23

Rule substitution questions are easier than they seem. There are not many ways the testmakers can create the same effect with a new rule.

Usually, the testmakers will use the secondary effects of a rule. For instance, in this case, rule 1 says that FH are together. So when rule 4 forces H to go into T, really it means that *FH* must go to T.

This means that you can duplicate the rule's effect by referring to F instead of H. Only **C** mentions F.

If you look closely, the effect is the same. Instead of forcing H and M into T, K forces *F* and M into T if K isn't assigned to T. Because F and H go together, this new rule forces H into T as well. **C is CORRECT.**

All of the wrong answers make one of these two mistakes:

- They allow things that aren't normally allowed.
- They ban things that aren't normally banned.

Some of the wrong answers are *true* according to the normal rules. But you're not looking for what's true. You're looking for something to replace the effect of the missing rule.

A is wrong because it allows one of H or M to be assigned to S with K. Normally this can't happen.

B is wrong because it doesn't say where F, H and M must go.

D is wrong because it doesn't force M to be assigned to T if K isn't assigned to T.

E is wrong because it should have said "unless *both* H and M are assigned...."

Section III – Reading Comprehension
Passage 1 – Perfumes
Questions 1–8

-- | --

Paragraph Summaries

1. Why isn't great perfume considered to be serious art form?
2. Perfumes are similar to other arts. Painting combines natural and synthetic ingredients, just like perfumes do. Oil paintings used subtle materials and changed over time.
3. Great perfumes are similarly subtle, and experienced noses can create imaginary worlds in their perfumes.
4. Corporations cheapen perfume recipes to make profits. This may be one reason why perfumes are not taken seriously.

Analysis

This is an interesting passage about perfume. I have a lousy sense of smell, so I hadn't even thought about whether perfume should be an art form. This passage makes a good case that perfume can reach the same aesthetic heights that other arts do.

The passage has a lot of small details you don't really need to know. The most important thing is to know *where* the details are. So if, for example, a question asks something about oil painting, you know to look at the second paragraph.

Your more important job is to understand what the author thinks and why they tell us the things they do. The main idea is that the author truly likes perfumes. They consider them an art form as cultivated as painting, architecture, music, etc. (lines 7-10)

As such, perfume is worthy of analysis. Paragraphs 2 and 3 are an argument aimed at demonstrating that perfumes can be great art. The author tells us about oil painting in paragraph 2, then uses paragraph 3 to show how complex great perfumes can be.

The fourth paragraph offers one explanation why perfumes are ignored. The author has shown that it's *possible* to create wonderful perfumes. However, most perfumes are not wonderful. Perfume manufacturers tamper with the ingredients to save money, and so most commercial perfumes fail to reach their potential.

Question 1

DISCUSSION: To answer main point questions, you have to ask "why is the author telling me this?". Pretend the author is a real person (they are!) and think about why they're saying the things they do.

The author's point is to convince us that perfumes can be great works of art. See lines 1-12, 37-44 and 44-45.

On main point questions, you can first eliminate answers that aren't even true, according to the passage. Truth doesn't guarantee an answer is correct, but it's necessary.

I'll note that I don't prephrase main point answers. I have a general sense of what the author thinks, but there are always 1,001 ways you could phrase it. So I wait to see what answer matches my general sense.

———————————

A. This isn't even true. Only paragraph 4 mentions corporations, and the author doesn't say a kind word about them.
B. This isn't necessarily true. The point of the first paragraph is that, for some reason, art experts *don't* focus attention on masterwork perfumes.
C. The author's argument is that perfumes should be taken seriously. They spend the passage asking why perfume isn't take seriously. The fact that perfumes are under corporate control is one possible reason that perfumes are ignored, but the main point itself is that perfumes should be given respect.
D. **CORRECT.** See the analysis above. The first paragraph sets the tone of the argument. The author is arguing that perfume deserves to be taken seriously.
E. This is just evidence supporting the author's argument that perfume should be taken seriously.

Question 2

DISCUSSION: The author mentions perfume recipes in paragraph 3. The recipes are very complex. Presumably, once a perfume is a masterpiece, the recipe shouldn't be altered. That would be as bad as editing one of Michelangelo's paintings to suit modern styles.

The author mentions perfume modification, negatively, in paragraph 4. Perfume manufacturers have changed many classic recipes for the worse.

While the author wouldn't want an original recipe change, he might accept a modification that brought one of those classic perfumes back to its original perfection.

———————————

A. Don't be fooled. The author likes *Joy Parfum*, but that doesn't mean that all perfume recipes would be improved by changing them to resemble *Joy Parfum*.
   That would be like modifying Picasso's paintings to make them look like Da Vinci's. A bad idea.
B. The author *dislikes* modifications that get rid of costly but essential ingredients. See paragraph 4.
C. This sounds tempting, but the author doesn't think that perfumes should be all natural. Lines 17-18 show that good perfumes should have some synthetic ingredients.
D. The author is interested in great art. Great art isn't necessarily popular. Art criticism is an elite activity and doesn't base itself on popular appeal.
E. **CORRECT.** This fits with paragraph 4. The authors disapproves of the way that corporations modified classic perfumes by using cheaper ingredients. So the author is likely to approve of any modification that reverses those changes.

Question 3

DISCUSSION: Questions with specific line references are easy. The only advice I can give you is to read the *entire* sentence and its context.

Here, line 29-31 says that "noses....*produce*" perfumes. So noses in this context are talented perfume makers.

I will admit that the sentence is very complex. The subject (noses) and the relevant verb (produce) are two lines apart! Looking for the subject and verb of every sentence helps break down complex LSAT sentences. This sentence is technically a compound sentence with two subjects for the verb: "Noses experiment....and produce". That subject and those two verbs are the core of the sentence.

_____

A. CORRECT. See the analysis above. If you read the entire sentence starting on line 29 and look for the verb, you'll see that noses produce perfumes.

B. The passage doesn't even mention perfume collectors.

C. How could a perfume be a nose? That's ridiculous. Besides, the sentence says that "noses experiment". A perfume can't experiment. The sentence is referring to humans.

D. The passage never mentions people who market perfumes.

E. The passage never mentions how perfumes are priced.

Question 4

DISCUSSION: There's nothing you can do to prepare for this type of question, since it gives you no prompt.

Instead, just keep an open mind as you look over the answers. Don't get stuck on one answer before you've looked at all of them.

And try to justify the right answer using the passage. If you've got a clear idea of the structure of the passage, you should be able to find the relevant line in 3-5 seconds. Finding lines is a skill you can improve if you practice it.

Note that three of the wrong answers are *extreme* general statements. They would be crazy statements if you applied them to real life. If you choose an incredibly extreme answer that seems to contradict reality, you need *very* clear backing from the passage. Extreme statements must be taken literally. If an answer says "all art" then that includes every art form on earth, past and present, large and small.

_____

A. CORRECT. Lines 37-43 say this directly.

B. Notice that this says *any* work of art. That's a very extreme view. There may be some type of art (wood engraving?) that doesn't produce small sensations combined harmoniously.

C. Like B, this is an extreme example. It says it's *utterly impossible* to make good art if you do it for commercial reasons. That's ridiculous. Much great art was created for commercial patrons. The passage would never suggest something that so blatantly contradicts reality.

D. The author didn't say this either. The author did say that oil paintings changes over time (lines 25-28), but they didn't say that oil paintings necessarily improve. Further, this question talks about *all* art. That's an extreme statement, and the passage makes no such general statements about *all* art forms.

E. The author doesn't say this. All they say is that perfume is a valid art form and deserves as much attention as the others. The author doesn't get into the business of ranking art beyond that.

Question 5

DISCUSSION: Note that this question is asking what the author "most likely" believes. As such, you don't need an answer that's 100% supported by the passage. You just need to find something that's probably true.

The author's main opinion is that perfumes can be great works of art and are worthy of analysis. This supports answer B: we have every reason to think that the author believes perfumes can be just as exquisite as statues. Line 12 says that *Joy Parfum* is a masterpiece. We have no reason to think that the author believes that masterpiece perfumes are any less important than other masterful works of art.

Note that we know *nothing* about *Joy Parfum* except that it is a masterpiece. (line 12)

———————————

A. Lines 10-12 say that art experts *do not* seek out *Joy Parfum*. So the passage somewhat contradicts this answer.
B. CORRECT. This is fairly well supported. The author thinks that perfumes are as important as other works of art (lines 37-43). And *Joy Parfum* is a masterpiece (line 12). So it's a fair assumption that the author thinks a masterpiece perfume is just as important as a great sculpture.
C. Let's not go too far. The author only said that *Joy Parfum* is a masterpiece. It's possible for an era to produce multiple masterworks. There may have been an even more important perfume than *Joy Perfume*. If I say "Jane is a wonderful person" it doesn't mean I think she's the *best* person in the world.
D. I was tempted by this, but there's no evidence for it. The passage doesn't say that *anyone* seeks out *Joy Parfum*. All we know is that art experts (who presumably have refined taste) do not seek out *Joy Parfum* (lines 10-12).
So we have zero evidence to suggest any group tends to like or dislike *Joy Parfum,* since no one appears to be seeking it out.
E. The author never said what *Joy Perfum's* formula was like, or if other perfumes of the same era had similar formulas.

Question 6

DISCUSSION: When a question mentions a specific line, you should go back and read the entire section for context.

Here, "cynical bean counters" are corporate managers. They change classic perfume recipes to use cheaper ingredients. Profits are higher, but quality is worse and the perfumes in question are no longer great art.

To parallel this, look for someone who makes something worse, in order to profit. Like perfume manufacturers, they will hope no one will notice their changes.

———————————

A. Popular tastes aren't necessarily bad. And this answer doesn't mention trying to save money.
B. CORRECT. This matches. Movies can be art. Here, the restrictions seem likely to lower the quality of the director's art in order to save money.
C. This is similar, but not the same. Corporations cut perfume costs in order to *increase profit*. They weren't forced to do this, they just wanted more money.
Whereas here the art institute has no choice. Revenues are likely to decline, so presumably they must cut costs or go bankrupt.
Note: You could of course construct an elaborate scenario where revenue declines but cuts aren't yet necessary and the director is using it as an excuse, etc. etc. But the principle of charity, which the LSAT uses, directs us not to think the worst of people. The director doesn't seem to be acting maliciously, so we should not strain ourselves to assume they're evil.
D. This isn't a bad thing. It's true the business executive's motives are commercial, but it doesn't sound like they're harming art. Whereas perfume company executives were destroying perfume for profit.
E. It sounds like the art dean is taking advantage of their position, but they aren't necessarily harming art. Perhaps their pet project is good art. Whereas the perfume company executives were *definitely* making perfumes worse.
Also, the art dean's motives are not commercial.

Question 7

DISCUSSION: This question asks about the final paragraph. You should reread that paragraph before answering a question like this. The paragraph is short, and rereading is *much* faster than reading the first time. You can probably reread it in 10 seconds, and then you'll have *all* the relevant information fresh in your mind as you answer.

The final paragraph says that perfume executives are cheapening classic perfume recipes so that they can make more profits. This is one possible reason that perfumes are not taken seriously as an art form.

A. The final paragraph only mentions customers to say that perfume executives hope that customers won't notice the recipes are worse (lines 52-54). There is zero support for the idea that customers don't know the names of perfumes.
B. CORRECT. This is likely true. The perfume executives have made perfumes *worse* while *increasing* profits. So it seems as though profits may actually be a reverse indicator.
C. This doesn't have to be true. Modern perfumes are worse, but maybe customers don't actually care.
D. We don't know anything about past perfumers. The fact that current perfume makers are bad doesn't mean that past perfume makers were good. And "never" tamper is a very strong statement. All it would take is *one* example of past tampering to disprove this answer.
E. This isn't supported at all. The author never mentions perfume price ranges. Perfumes cost less to produce, but that tells us nothing about how much perfumes are sold for.

Question 8

DISCUSSION: This question asks about the organization of the passage. Before looking at the answers, you should skim over each paragraph and decide upon a short summary.

Here's mine: The first paragraph asks why perfume is not taken more seriously. The second and third paragraphs explain why perfume ought to be taken seriously. The final paragraph gives one possible reason why perfume is not taken seriously.

You can use this summary to eliminate answers. Be ruthless. A single error in an answer means that you can discard it and move on to better candidates.

A. The first paragraph does more than make an observation. Instead, it asks a question: why isn't perfume art? The second and third cases present an argument that perfume *should* be art. This answer instead presents very neutral language for the second and third paragraphs: "elaborate on the observation"....that phrase doesn't describe an argument.
B. The fourth paragraph doesn't reject a challenge to the idea that perfumes are art. Instead, the fourth paragraph gives an explanation for why perfumes are ignored.
C. The second and third paragraphs aren't a response to the claim that perfumes are art. Instead, they're an argument supporting the idea that perfumes are art.
D. CORRECT. This matches the description above. "Helps to justify the posing of the question" is a fancy way of saying that the second and third paragraphs support the idea that perfumes should be considered art. (The original question was: why aren't perfumes art? By presenting a case that perfumes are art, the second and third paragraphs show that this was a reasonable question to ask.)
E. The second and third paragraphs don't present any consequences. Instead, they're arguments supporting the idea that perfumes are art.

Passage 2 – Stealing Thunder
Questions 9–16

Paragraph Summaries

1. "Stealing thunder" is a legal strategy that involves revealing damaging information about one client. This is only done if the information was already likely to be revealed by the opposition.
2. **Paragraph 2, part 1:** Mock trials and psychological experiments support the idea that stealing thunder is effective. For instance, revealing damaging information may boost credibility and allow jurors to form counterarguments against the opposition's case.
   Paragraph 2, part 2: Scarce information is more valuable. If both sides mention damaging information, then that information will seem less important.
3. Stealing thunder also allows lawyers to frame negative information with "spin". But this only works if the negative information isn't too damaging. Otherwise, revealing information can give a jury a negative view of your case.

Analysis

There is a *lot* of information in the second paragraph. Don't just skim over it. If you don't understand something or feel you forgot information, reread that section.

Rereading is a lot faster than reading the first time, and it vastly increases your retention and understanding of the passage. This in turn lets you solve questions much faster and avoid trap answers. So rereading probably increases overall speed by reducing your time spent on the questions.

This passage is about the legal tactic "stealing thunder". This tactic's name comes from an english idiom. If, for example, a friend announces your wedding before you do, then your friend stole your thunder.

Any trial will include some information that harms your case. You might think it best to wait for the opposition to reveal this information. But the first paragraph actually says that many lawyers prefer to reveal damaging information themselves.

No researchers have studied the effectiveness of stealing thunder directly (see lines 11-12). But some mock trial studies and unrelated psychological studies show why stealing thunder may be an effective tactic.

Not much attention is given to simulated trials. These are only mentioned on lines (13-20). We know that stealing thunder was effective in these mock trials – we are given no further details.

Lines 18 to the end of the passage discuss psychological studies that show why stealing thunder may be effective. I'll sum up the reasons:

Credibility: Volunteering damaging information can make you more credible. See lines 20-25.
Counterarguments: If you volunteer damaging information first, and present it positively, jurors may counterarguments against claims the opposition will make later. See lines 25-33.
Scarcity: Having both sides mention a damaging fact makes the information more common and therefore less valuable. See lines 33-43.
Spin: If information isn't too negative, you can cast it in a positive light. See lines 44-54.

The author also points out some negative consequences of stealing thunder. If information is incredibly damaging to your case, it may be better to wait. Presenting strongly negative information early may bias the jurors against you. See lines 54-59 and lines 42-43.

I'll repeat that *no* researchers have directly studied the effectiveness of "stealing thunder" in actual trials. This is an extremely important fact, and knowing this lets you eliminate many wrong answers.

Question 9

DISCUSSION: To prepare for main point questions, you should always ask yourself "why is the author telling me this?". Pretend they're a real person, talking to you.

Lines 11-15 are key. They show that the point of the article is to discuss how certain studies indicate that "stealing thunder" can be an effective tactic.

———————————

A. This answer is false. Lines 11-12 say that stealing thunder's effectiveness in actual trials has never been studied.
B. The passage never mentions "predicting jurors' attitudes". This answer is designed to mislead you. The only negative to stealing thunder is if the information is very important, see lines 54-59.
C. **CORRECT.** This covers the whole passage. Paragraph 1 shows that lawyers believe in the effectiveness of stealing thunder. Lines 11-20 show that the rest of the passage will be about the psychological evidence that supports stealing thunder.

This answer doesn't mention the negative effects in paragraph 4, but a main point answer doesn't have to include every bit of information that's in a passage.
D. This doesn't match the passage. The passage said that making information readily available was an *advantage* of stealing thunder. See lines 33-43. If information is widely available, it will be judged to be less important.
E. This is too strong. First, most of the research was psychological research. It was not designed to test stealing thunder's effectiveness.

Second, there hasn't been any direct research testing stealing thunder's effectiveness in courtrooms (lines 10-11). So we can't say that stealing thunder has been "vindicated". The research merely *supports* the idea that stealing thunder works.

Question 10

DISCUSSION: Lines 1-4 define stealing thunder. It's when you reveal negative information about your own client before the opposition has a chance to.

———————————

A. This reveals information about the opposition. Stealing thunder is about revealing information about *your own* client.
B. **CORRECT.** This matches exactly. The lawyer is revealing mildly negative information about their own client before the opposition has a chance to.
C. Stealing thunder is when you reveal information *before* the opposition does. In this case, the lawyer is only admitting to information *after* the opposition revealed it.
D. There's no information revealed here. If you attack the reasoning in someone's argument, you aren't necessarily adding any new facts.
E. Stealing thunder is about revealing information. Here, the lawyer has revealed no information.

Question 11

DISCUSSION: The question says the answer is *literally mentioned* in the passage. So to be sure about questions like these, check the passage to make certain your answer is there. If you have a good mental map of the passage, you should be able to find a specific reference in 3-5 seconds. If you can't do this, practice doing it faster.

All of the wrong answers are things that make sense as being factors....but they're not mentioned in the passage. Common sense can be helpful in evaluating answers, but you can't use common sense to choose an answer that was totally absent from the passage.

_____

A. This sounds like it might be a good idea, but the passage never mentions it.
B. The passage never mentions lawyer skill as a factor.
C. The passage never mentioned having clients testify in person about mistakes.
D. CORRECT. Lines 50-54 say this directly. As long as the information isn't too negative, stealing thunder can help guide jurors' views.
E. The passage never mentions jury selection.

Question 12

DISCUSSION: See lines 50-59 for a full discussion of this cognitive framework. Basically, at the start of a trial jurors have zero information. They want context that will let them interpret the facts they hear. The first lawyer to present information has a chance to frame how jurors view that information and all later testimony.

So stealing thunder can help present a positive mental model for jurors, as you have the chance to frame how they view the information. But if the information is *too* negative, then early exposure may backfire, as jurors will form a negative mental model.

So "cognitive framework" just refers to the initial information that will let jurors decide how to interpret later facts.

_____

A. CORRECT. Lines 50-54 say this directly. If you present information early on, with a positive frame, this will affect how jurors interpret later information.
B. This isn't what lines 50-59 say. This answer is *true* in real life, but you're not looking for something that's true. You're looking for something that answers the question asked.
C. The amount of impact isn't the key. The point of the cognitive framework is that if you frame damaging evidence positively, the information may even have a *positive* impact. There's a lot of power in being able to create a mental framework for jurors to use.
D. This contradicts lines 50-59. In cases where information is too negative, stealing thunder should either be done very late or not at all. Overly negative information early on can bias the jury against you.
E. This doesn't match the passage. The author never compared creating credibility vs. positive framing. Credibility was only mentioned on line 21, it had nothing to do with the cognitive framework on lines 50-59.

Question 13

DISCUSSION: *All* of the wrong answers are never mentioned in the passage. Instead, they're things you associate with courtrooms from your background knowledge.

Background knowledge can help orient your thinking, but it can *never* be used to justify an answer on a question like this. Check the passage to confirm your choice. If you don't, you're likely to fall into a trap.

———————————

A. The author never mentions this fear. In fact, in lines 13-15, the author states that stealing thunder is generally effective.
B. The author never said that stealing thunder should only be used in opening statements. In fact, opening statements are not mentioned even once in the passage.
C. The author didn't mention anecdotes even once. This answer is trying to mislead you by alluding to the dangers of stealing thunder mentioned in lines 50-59, but that section had nothing to do with anecdotes.
D. CORRECT. Lines 11-20 say this more or less directly.
E. The passage never mentions courtroom experience.

Question 14

DISCUSSION: Lines 10-11 say that there has been no research of stealing thunder's effectiveness in actual trials. This fact eliminates *all* the wrong answers.

———————————

A. The passage never mentions any surveys of lawyers, and lines 10-11 say there have been no actual legal studies of stealing thunder's effectiveness. Though the second half of this answer is right; there were studies on simulated trials (see lines 13-14).
B. The passage said there have been *no* studies of stealing thunder's effectiveness in actual trials. See lines 11-12.
C. The first half of this is wrong. Lines 11-12 say that there have been no studies of stealing thunder's effectiveness in actual trials.
D. Lines 11-12 say there have been no studies of stealing thunder's effectiveness in actual trials. And I have no idea what the first half of this refers to: the passage never mentioned anything "analogous" to stealing thunder.
E. CORRECT. This matches. Specifically, this refers to the simulated trials and the psychological research in lines 11-20. The psychological research supports the use of stealing thunder, but the research itself wasn't law-related.

Question 15

DISCUSSION: Lines 6-10 offer a summary of the benefits of stealing thunder. The author says, in line 14, that stealing thunder is effective.

The author couldn't be referring to a definition of stealing thunder that they hadn't yet stated, so the claim on line 14 can only be interpreted in reference to the earlier definition of stealing thunder in lines 6-10. That definition is the basis of answer A.

———————

A. **CORRECT.** This is the best answer. Stealing thunder offers no guarantee of victory, but it does generally improve how jurors view negative information. Lines 6-10 summarize this rationale.

B. This is a misstatement of lines 26-30. Those lines said that, once lawyers introduce information, jurors will use that information to form counterarguments. So the *jurors* make up counterarguments – lawyers don't supply the counterarguments.

C. This is far too strong. Lines 10-11 say we don't even have courtroom evidence of the effectiveness of stealing thunder. And even if it works, stealing thunder certainly doesn't guarantee victory. It merely reduces the impact of negative information, but the information is still negative.

D. Hogwash. The passage doesn't mention "forcefully capturing" attention or getting juries to focus more attentively. This answer has nothing to do with what's said in the passage.

E. Lines 10-11 say we have *no* studies of the effectiveness of stealing thunder in actual courtrooms. So we definitely don't know if this answer choice is true.

Question 16

DISCUSSION: Lawyers' attitudes are only mentioned in lines 6-10. Lawyers think that, *if information is likely to be revealed by the opposition,* then lawyers should instead reveal it themselves.

If negative information isn't likely to be revealed, then there's no point to bringing it up.

Since this is literally the only thing we know about lawyer's opinions on when to steal thunder, it *has* to be the right answer.

———————

A. This is something *the author* believes, based on lines 50-59. But the passage never said *lawyers* think this. Lawyers' opinions are only given on lines 6-10.

B. This is never mentioned, and also vague. This says "some" of the facts. That's a very low bar. If jurors know the name of the accused, then they technically know "some" of the facts. That's a pretty useless basis upon which to decide whether to steal thunder.
This answer does *not* say that a decision to steal thunder should depend on whether jurors already know the negative fact in question, which may have been how you interpreted it. That could have been the right answer, but that's not what this answer says.

C. This is simply never mentioned in the passage.

D. **CORRECT.** See the analysis above.

E. The question asks what lawyers believe. This can't be the right answer, because we don't know what lawyers think about psychological studies. Only the author mentions psychological studies.

Passage 3 – Neuroscience and Free Will (comparative)
Questions 17–21

Paragraph Summaries

Passage A

1. Neuroscience says we may be acting emotionally even if we think we're rational.
2. So we should stop punishing people for crimes. Instead, we should only use jail time to try to deter crimes.

Passage B

1. Neuroscience shows our actions are determined in advance by the physics of our brains.
2. Nonetheless, Alfred J. Ayer argues that free will is possible.
3. Our actions are free if they're the product of a healthy brain and we face no outside constraint.

Analysis

The passages aren't complex, but they have some concepts that are hard to understand.

The point of the first passage is that neuroscience shows that we are not rational. Brain scans show that our decisions are made by our emotions, even when we think we're acting rationally. (lines 9-14)

Lines 15-24 show how this should affect our criminal sentencing. Currently, we have at least two reasons for sentencing people to jail:

Retribution: Retribution is punishment for acts that we think are wrong. If someone murders another person, we think that action is wrong. So we send the murdered to jail to punish them for doing a bad thing.

Deterrence: We don't want murders to happen. If there's a strong jail term for murder, then people will think twice before committing murder.

We currently use both retribution and deterrence as justifications for sending people to jail. It's important to think of them both separately. This makes the argument in the passage clearer. The author is *not* saying we should get rid of jail. They're saying we should no longer use *punishment* as a reason for sending people to jail.

This is hard to think about, because in popular narratives, punishment is the main reason we think of when we consider criminal sentencing. People want criminals to suffer for the bad things they do.

Passage A is saying that this is *not* a good reason to send people to jail. Neuroscience shows that we are not responsible for our actions, and so we should not jail people in order to punish them. We should, therefore, only jail people in order to deter crimes.

I personally think this is a silly argument. It may philosophically be true that we have no free will. But we live our lives as if we do. So I don't think we ought to do away with the concept of free will in practice merely because on an atomic level it doesn't hold true.

But that's beside the point. The main things you should take out of passage A are as follows:

- We don't control our actions rationally.
- Retribution jails people to punish them.
- Deterrence jails people to prevent crimes.
- Since people don't commit crimes rationally, we shouldn't jail them for punishment. Only deterrence is a good motive.

Passage B discusses the ideas of an English philosopher, Alfred J. Ayer. The author of passage B agrees that we don't control our actions. This is referred to as determinism.

Yet Ayer argues free will is still a useful concept. He distinguishes between actions that have external constraints vs. those that don't.

For example, suppose someone sticks a gun to your back and asks for your wallet. You hand it over. Your action was not free: you had a strong internal reason to give the robber your wallet.

Now suppose someone walks up to you and nicely asks for your wallet. You are free to decide (most people would decide "no").

It is true that your answer in a "free" situation is already determined by the chemistry of your brain. But since the deciding factors were internal, we can fairly call this decision free.

Mental illness is a distinguishing factor. If you have a mental disease, then your actions may not be free. Lines 38-43 discuss mental disorders.

The author of passage B appears to agree with Ayers' argument. In lines 53-56 the author extends Ayers' argument to define when actions are free: When there is no external constraint, and the brain is healthy.

Question 17

DISCUSSION: The two passages don't overlap much. Passage B doesn't talk about justice or punishment.

Three wrong answers mention jail. They're all wrong for the same reason: Passage B doesn't mention punishment.

The two passages only overlap in that they both talk about neuroscience and its implications for free will. See lines 1-3, 9-14 and lines 25-29.

A. Passage B doesn't discuss punishment or jail.
B. **CORRECT.** See the lines quoted above.
C. Passage B doesn't discuss punishment or jail.
D. Passage B doesn't discuss punishment or jail.
E. Passage A doesn't discuss constraints on actions. Outside physical force as a cause for our actions was only discussed in passage B, line 44.

Question 18

DISCUSSION: To be clear, you're looking for something that's *in* passage B, and *not in* passage A. So you can eliminate an answer if it fails to meet either condition.

Two answers (D and E) aren't in either passage. One answer, B, is in passage A, so it's out. C is tricky, I've discussed it in more depth below.

A. **CORRECT.** Only passage B mentions mental disorder. See lines 39 and 55.
B. Line 10 in passage A mentions free choice.
C. This is a tricky answer. Line 28 in passage B does say "causally", and the term is absent from Passage A. So superficially this seems correct.
   But this answer is wrong for two reasons:
   1. Even though the term "causally" is absent from passage A, the concept of causation is still important. Causality really just means: what makes things happen. And Passage A is definitely about that: the author debates whether our actions are caused by our will or our emotions.
   2. Second, although "causally" is mentioned in passage B, this term is not really part of the argument. The term was just used to give an intro to the passage and state that we live in a deterministic world. Passage B's argument itself is only from lines 32-56, *after* causally is mentioned. So the appearance of the term "causally" has no real significance for the argument.
D. Self-delusion isn't mentioned in either passage.
E. Passage B doesn't mention moral responsibility. Passage A mentions moral choice, but that's a different concept.

Question 19

DISCUSSION: Hume was a famous and respected philosopher. By mentioning that Hume and Ayer agree, the author lends credibility to Ayer's argument.

A. Not so. It's an insult to say that someone is not an original thinker. The author *agrees* with Ayer, so there's no reason the author would try to insult Ayer.
   While Hume argued something similar to Ayer, it seems as though Ayer has produced a theory that has new details. If Ayer had no new ideas, the author would have just discussed Hume directly.
B. **CORRECT.** David Hume is a famous, respected philosopher. By suggesting that Hume agrees with Ayer, the author lends respect to Ayer's theory.
C. Nonsense. If you read everything in context, it's clear that the author is discussing the present, not the past. The author of passage B makes no reference to the past apart from mentioning David Hume.
D. This is wrong for two reasons. First, while Hume agrees we can be free in a deterministic world, that's not necessarily the same thing as "soft determinism". Soft determinism is Ayer's theory. Secondly, Ayer invented soft determinism in 1954. Mechanistic ideas appear to have been around before that.
E. The author did *not* say that neuroscientists are wrong to describe the brain mechanistically. The author merely thinks that determinism and free will aren't contradictory concepts; see lines 29-31. In other words, the brain acts mechanistically, but we can still call ourselves free.

Question 20

DISCUSSION: I found this question difficult. I had to go by process of elimination. I had to consider the question at length on review to get a better understanding of why the right answer is right.

I now see that certain keywords show that passage A is considerably more in favor of the ideas it discusses than passage B.

Both authors agree with what they are discussing. But passage A is more forceful. On line 4, the author says that new findings "radically" change how we should think about the law.

Lines 15-20 say that this new idea should lead us to abandon the now dominant idea of retribution in criminal sentencing. In other words, the author of passage A is so committed to the ideas they're discussing that they recommend completely changing our legal system and how we think about crime. That's a major suggestion!

Whereas the author of passage B only speaks mildly favorably of Ayer. In lines 52-56 they extend Ayer's ideas, showing that they do agree with Ayer. But they agree with Ayer without any hyperbolic terms like "radical", and they don't suggest dramatic changes in our institutions as a result of these ideas.

So **C**, "detached", is the best answer: the author of passage A more closely associates themselves with the ideas they discuss than the author of passage B does. "Engaged" was the other answer I considered, but to be engaged with ideas is just to actively consider the ideas you're discussing, and both authors do that.

Neither author is skeptical or dismissive (they're similar terms), and they're definitely not ironic.

———————

A. See the analysis above.
B. The author of passage B agrees with Ayer. See lines 52-56, where the author even extends Ayer's ideas.
C. CORRECT. See the analysis above.
D. Irony is notoriously hard to define. This is highly unlikely to ever be an LSAT answer.
E. Same as B.

Question 21

DISCUSSION: In passage A, the author argues that new findings in neuroscience show that we've been doing criminal law all wrong. We should completely change how we punish crimes. See lines 3-5 and lines 15-20.

To find an analogous argument, look for a situation where new information should change how we do things. The right answer doesn't have to mention crime or rationality. The point of an analogy is that the subject matter can be completely different.

———————

A. The author wasn't arguing that we should simplify law.
B. This does talk about rationality. But an analogy doesn't need to use the same subject matter! This still could have been the right answer if it had said "thus, we should change our economic institutions". Instead, this merely says we won't make good predictions.
C. CORRECT. This is the best match. It doesn't matter that this answer didn't mention rationality. The central element of the passage is that new information shows our existing theories are completely wrong and we must change how we do things as a result.
D. This is just a random argument about when civil disobedience is allowed. There are no new finding or any recommended changes to a social system.
E. This is just a definition of autonomy. There are no new findings or recommended changes.

Passage 4 – Mexican Americans (Garcia)
Questions 22–27

Paragraph Summaries

1. Garcia argues that earlier Mexican American activists were more diverse and radical than previously thought. But Garcia's work is flawed.
2. Oddly, Garcia argues that the diverse groups had much consensus. This is wrong.
3. It's unclear how representative Mexican American political leaders were of the Mexican American population as a whole.

Analysis

This is one of the most complex reading comprehension passages I've ever seen. Trust me, everything in this essay makes sense and has real meaning – the LSAT doesn't use vague nonsense language. But though this passage has real meaning, it's hard nonetheless. I'm going to summarize and simplify it.

Garcia says:

- Mexican American activists from 1930-60 were diverse.
- These early activists were more radical than believed.
- There was consensus in the Mexican American activity community (paragraph 2)
- The activists were representative of the Mexican American population. (Paragraph 3)

The author of the passage agrees with the first two points. They think Garcia is wrong on the third and fourth points.

In the second paragraph, the author argues that Garcia is inconsistent. Garcia argues that there was a consensus among Mexican American activists. This contrasts with Garcia's view that the movement had great diversity.

The second paragraph describes two different groups: the League of United Latin American Citizens and the Congress of Spanish-Speaking People.

The first group thoughts Mexican Americans should assimilate. The second group wanted separate cultures and bilingual schooling.

Garcia argued that both groups were united in favor of liberal reform. But the author points out that there were intense debates within the Mexican American community, and therefore no real consensus. (See lines 30-36)

So to sum up the second paragraph: Garcia's views on diversity and consensus are inconsistent, and also incorrect, as there was no real consensus.

The third paragraph is more complex. In this paragraph, we see Garcia's view that the Mexican American activists were representative of the Mexican American population at the time. That is to say that Garcia believes the Mexican American population was just as radical as its representatives.

To support this, Garcia noted that the *leaders* had increasingly grown up in American culture, and had absorbed the liberal slogans of World War II.

The author says that this evidence about the leaders tells us anything about the population as a whole. Garcia's only evidence is that the proportion of Mexican Americans born in America had increased. That is to say, a greater percentage of Mexican Americans were born in the United States.

In lines 53-60, the author essentially says that the issue is complicated. There are a bunch of factors at work, and we don't know how they affected the attitudes of ordinary Mexican Americans. We can't automatically assume that the attitudes of Mexican American leaders were shared by the people.

Question 22

DISCUSSION: The League of United Latin American Citizens and the Congress of Spanish Speaking People are mentioned on lines 18-26.

The League favored assimilation with America. The Congress wanted to keep the two cultures separate, and favored more rights for Mexicans along with bilingual education.

This question is asking what the League believed. So the answer will almost certainly be about assimilation. See lines 18-22.

———————

A. The passage never mentions what other United States Citizens believed. We only know about Mexican American groups.
B. This is what the Congress believes, see lines 22-26.
C. The author never says precisely what the League thought about immigration. According to line 29, *both* groups favored liberal reform. We know the League and the Congress fought about immigration (lines 30-32), but we don't know which one favored a more liberal policy.
D. This sounds like something the Congress believed. The League believed in assimilation, which would involve speaking English. See lines 18-22.
E. **CORRECT.** Lines 18-22 say this: the League favored assimilation. Assimilation means adopting the culture of the country you've moved to.

Question 23

DISCUSSION: Many lines in the first and second paragraphs quote Garcia's opinions directly. So for this type of question you should look to justify the answer by finding a line in the passage. Garcia literally says the right answer.

———————

A. **CORRECT.** Lines 7-10 say this directly. Those lines mean that activists of the 1930-40s were proposing reforms similar to those in 1960-70.
B. Lines 4-5 show that Garcia thought the early activists were *more* diverse than has been acknowledged.
Garcia never compares the early activists to those of 1960-70, so we can't know his opinion on this question.
C. There's no evidence for this. Lines 7-10 suggest that Garcia thought the 1960-70 activists were more radical. (We can't be sure, since those lines are the author speaking. The main point is that we don't know Garcia's opinion of this answer choice.)
D. This is only true of the Congress of Spanish-Speaking People, lines 24-26. Garcia didn't say that most Mexican American political activists agreed with the Congress.
E. Actually, lines 26-30 say that Garcia thought all groups agreed on liberal reform as a goal.

Question 24

DISCUSSION: This is a hard question. It's best to justify your answer on a question like this using the passage. All of the wrong answers are designed to trap you into picking something that's similar to the passage, but was not in the passage.

Note that the question is asking what Garcia thought about Mexican Americans in general, not just the activists. Garcia's views on Mexican Americans in general are in paragraph 3, only.

Garcia thought that Mexican Americans as a whole were more politically engaged. Garcia's only evidence was that the *leaders* of the Mexican American community were more engaged and assimilated into US culture (lines 43-51).

A. The author mentions variations in ethnic consciousness on line 56 as an unknown factor. Garcia never mentioned this term.
B. **CORRECT.** Lines 40-46 say this. A higher proportion of Mexican Americans were born in America, and therefore they were more familiar with American culture. And the word acculturated on line 45 means "assimilated into the dominant culture".
C. Garcia believed the opposite of this. In lines 40-51, Garcia argues that assimilation *increased* political activity.
D. This is a trap answer. Line 49-51 say that leaders of the Mexican American community wanted to achieve full rights. But Garcia doesn't say they're militant. Militant is only used on line 10 to describe a different group of Mexican Americans, those from 1960-70.
E. This contradicts the passage. Line 48 says that the rhetoric of World War II was *inclusive*. That means America wanted to welcome all communities to be part of the US. WWII slogans were a positive thing, according to the passage!

Question 25

DISCUSSION: This question is asking for the author's opinion, not Garcia's opinion. Be careful not to choose something Garcia believes, since the author generally disagrees with Garcia.

A. On line 10, the author said that the activists of the 1960s-70s were more militant, but the author didn't say *why* they were. And further, on lines 28-36 the author disagreed that Mexican American groups were truly united by liberal reform.
B. **CORRECT.** Lines 28-36 say this directly. Garcia thinks that liberal reform unified Mexican Americans, but the author points to the debates among Mexican American groups as a sign that they weren't truly united.
C. This contradicts lines 28-36. The author believes the debates were so sharp that there was no consensus.
D. The author said that the Congress and the League (lines 18-24) had differing opinions, but the author didn't say how much support each group had.
E. The author didn't say this. On lines 28-36, the author says that Mexican American groups were divided. But they didn't say that this division caused problems.

Question 26

DISCUSSION: The author shows uncertainty in the third paragraph. They say we can't know what the Mexican American population believed, since we only have evidence about the leaders. See lines 51-60.

When you first read a passage, you should take careful note of an author's opinions, including things such as uncertainty. Then, if and when a question refers to that belief, you'll know where to look.

For a few answers, we may not know exactly what the author thinks. But that's not what we're looking for. We're looking for something where the author literally expresses uncertainty.

———————————

A. First, the short version. The author had a clear answer for the question in this answer choice: no, we can't know the effect of the increase. Lines 57-58 say this directly. The question was asking for uncertainty, but on this question the author is very sure that we can't know.
Proportion vs. Number: This answer makes a second, major error. This answer refers to the an increase in the *number* of Mexican Americans born in America. But the author only referred to the *proportion,* on line 41.
Number and proportion are two *very* different concepts. But they're often confused, and the LSAT mercilessly exploits this confusion.
An example of a number is: 5 million Mexican Americans born in the USA. An example of a proportion is: 45% of Mexican Americans were born in the USA.
Proportion is more relevant in assessing the beliefs of a community, since it refers to the total percent of a community that may share certain beliefs. Number is not the right term.
In any case, this answer would still be wrong, even if it had said number, because the author had no uncertainty on this issue. See lines 57-58.

B. The author doesn't express uncertainty about the historians, who are mentioned on line 5. It's true we don't know the author's precise opinion. But that's not what this question asked. We're looking for something where the author literally said: "I don't know".
C. The author has an answer to this question: no, there wasn't. See lines 30-36.
D. CORRECT. See lines 51-60, especially 51-52: "it is not clear how far....". On this issue, the author's opinion is that we can't know.
E. The author did not say "it is unclear how the league and the Congress" interacted.

Question 27

DISCUSSION: Ethnic consciousness is only mentioned on line 56. Lines 53-56 say that bilingualism and immigration rates affect ethnic consciousness, though we don't know how.

Any other answer is just nonsense intended to distract you.

A. Lines 53-56 say we *don't* know how immigration rates affect ethnic consciousness.

B. The passage never talks about the *number* of Mexicans born in the United States. The passage only talks about the *proportion* (e.g. 45%). Number and proportion are completely different. There's no support for this answer.
   Note: This answer would still have been wrong if it had said proportion. The passage never said whether the proportion born in the USA affects political consciousness. Lines 51-60 mention these terms, but they say we don't know how they're related.

C. Lines 51-60 say that we *don't* know if changes in political leadership reflected changes in the Mexican American population.

D. The passage *never* talks about what influence, if any, Mexican American leaders had over the Mexican American population. This answer has zero support.

E. **CORRECT.** Lines 53-56 say this. Variations in immigration affect ethnic consciousness, though we can't quite say how.

Section IV – Logical Reasoning

Question 1

QUESTION TYPE: Misinterpretation

ARGUMENTS: Ming says it's good that trans fats have generally been removed from cookies. Trans fats aren't healthy.

Carol doesn't understand Ming's argument. She accuses Ming of arguing that cookies are healthy.

ANALYSIS: Carol fails to understand Ming's argument. Notice that Carol says "Why do you say that?". She is utterly confused about the point of Ming's argument.

Ming's argument, better expressed, goes like this: If someone eats a cookie, it would be better for that cookies not to have trans fats. So it's good that cookies now don't have trans fats.

Ming isn't arguing that we should eat cookies. They're saying, *if* we do, then it's a good thing that the cookies don't have trans fats.

A lot of the wrong answers don't make sense in light of what Carol said in the stimulus. For an answer to be right, Carol's reply in the stimulus has to be something she would say in response to the belief stated in the answer choice.

_____

A. Neither Carol nor Ming talks about higher or lower levels of trans fats.
B. CORRECT. This must be how Carol interpreted Ming's argument. That's why Carol pointed out that desserts still aren't healthy.
C. This answer would only have made sense if Carol had said "Just because cookies aren't good for you, doesn't mean they're bad for you". But Carol never addressed the distinction between "not good (neutral)" and "bad".
D. This answer would have made sense if Carol had said "A cookie isn't healthy just because it has less trans fat. Any trans fat is dangerous."
E. This answer would have made sense if Carol had said something like: "It's possible consumers can still choose to purchase trans fat cookies if they accept the health risks."

Question 2

QUESTION TYPE: Identify the Conclusion

CONCLUSION: We shouldn't accept the "thrift and hard work" hypothesis for the success of the industrial revolution. We need historical evidence first.

REASONING: Successful explanations need to be based on facts.

ANALYSIS: Certain words indicate conclusions and premises. In the final sentence, "but" indicates that the author disagrees with what was said before. "So" introduces their conclusion.

For instance: John says we should buy the car. **But** it's too expensive, **so** we should look for a better deal.

But = contrasting evidence.
So = conclusion.

(These definitions are *generally* true. But it's possible for "so" not to be the conclusion in certain cases. Take the definitions above as rules of thumb.

_____

A. The productivity growth of the economy is what we're trying to explain. It's not the conclusion. The point of the argument is that we don't yet know how to explain this growth.
B. This is just context. The fact that productivity growth raised living standards explains why we care about the industrial revolution in the first place.
C. **CORRECT.** See the analysis above. The final sentence states this conclusion and the reason for it.
D. The historian didn't say that values were not the cause. The historian said that *we don't know* if values were the cause. It's possible they were – we just lack evidence.
E. This is just like D. The historian didn't say there was no shift in values. They said *we don't know* if there was a shift in values. It's possible that there was one.

Question 3

QUESTION TYPE: Strengthen

CONCLUSION: The donated trees are probably native trees that don't grow to be very large.

REASONING: The trees come from Three Rivers Nursery, which mostly sells native trees and shrubs.

ANALYSIS: There were two conditions in the master plan:

- The tree is native to the area.
- The tree doesn't grow very large.

The nursery mostly sells native trees and shrubs, so there's decent evidence the nursery's trees are probably native. But we don't know for sure. We only know that most *trees and shrubs* are native. But that could be mostly shrubs. For instance, this is a possible breakdown of the nursery's plants:

- 30% non-native trees.
- 10% native trees.
- 60% native shrubs.

In this example, most of the plants are either native trees or shrubs. But most of the trees are non-native. So we could strengthen the argument by showing that most of the trees themselves are native, which would eliminate possibilities like the one I described above.

The evidence is also missing the other condition. We don't know how large the nursery's native trees get. If many nursery trees grow large like cottonwoods do, then the donated trees are no good. We can strengthen the argument by showing the nursery's trees are small.

Note: It's not clear whether non-native trees are allowed. "Calls for" usually means that the rules listed are a complete expression of the plan. But it's possible other rules allow non-native trees. However, this doesn't matter, since we don't know what non-native trees comply with the master plan. The only way to prove that the nursery trees comply is for them to be native, since we know what conditions native trees must meet.

A. This answer must be talking about non-native trees. The master plan clearly said that large native trees are no good.
This answer can't strengthen anything, because it's so vague. It could mean that *one* type of non-native tree not carried by the nursery grows large and is consistent with the plan. That doesn't help prove anything about nursery trees.

B. This *weakens* the argument. Cottonwoods grow large, so they're not consistent with the master plan.

C. This weakens the argument. We only know that native trees are consistent with the master plan. This answer *lessens* the amount of native trees carried by the nursery. We know that most of what the nursery sells are native trees and shrubs. For instance, 60% of the stock is "native trees and shrubs". The greater percentage of that 60% that's shrubs, the smaller the percentage that's native trees.

D. This weakens the argument, because it *reduces* the amount of trees that are consistent with the plan. This answer makes it less likely that the nursery carried some allowable non-native trees.

E. **CORRECT.** This strengthens the argument. The plan doesn't allow trees that are too large. So this answer shows that the nursery's native trees will meet the plans requirements: they're native, and they don't grow too large.

Question 4

QUESTION TYPE: Necessary Assumption

CONCLUSION: *Diplodocus* surely ate ground plants or underwater plants.

REASONING: *Diplodocus* could have eaten ground plants. It couldn't have eaten tree plants by raising its neck.

ANALYSIS: This question plays the old trick of forcing your mind into a narrow frame. The author wants you to think that it's only possible for a *Diplodocus* to eat high plants by raising it's neck.

But there are other possibilities. The right answer shows that *Diplodocus* could have eaten high plants by standing on its hind legs.

_____

A. This strengthens the argument, but it's not necessary. *Diplodocus* could have eaten on the ground even if its neck was unique.
   Negation: No modern ground feeding animal had a neck like *Diplodocus*.
B. This is a side issue. We only care about whether the neck went downwards while feeding. It doesn't matter whether *Diplodocus* raised its head to a neutral position when it wasn't feeding.
   Negation: *Diplodocus* fed on the ground, but raised its head to a neutral position when it wasn't eating, and it could see fine.
C. This doesn't matter. We already know that the neck structure of *Diplodocus* made it impossible for it to raise its head. This answer just adds a superfluous second reason that head raising wouldn't work.
   Negation: *Diplodocus* could supply blood to a raised head, but it couldn't raise its head due to neck issues.
D. **CORRECT.** The negation of this answer wrecks the argument. If there are other ways of eating high vegetation, then *Diplodocus* might not have eaten from the ground.
   Negation: *Diplodocus* had other ways of reaching high growing vegetation.
E. The argument is trying to prove that *Diplodocus* ate ground and underwater vegetation. This answer *weakens* the argument by reducing the possibilities for eating water vegetation.

Question 5

QUESTION TYPE: Principle–Justify

CONCLUSION: The government shouldn't rebuild the trails that were destroyed by a landslide.

REASONING: Future landslides could hurt people.

ANALYSIS: Principle questions test your ability to separate facts from morality. You can't assume *any* moral principles on the LSAT, even ones as commonly accepted as "it is a bad thing for people to die".

There are good reasons for this. Any action carries risks, even risk of death. That's not necessarily a reason to avoid doing something. Maybe the benefits outweigh the risk. In the face of risks, we need to explicitly state the principles that govern our choices.

To strengthen this argument, we should say that the government shouldn't support construction where there is a risk of death by landslide.

_____

A. The argument did *not* say that the government should ban the community from rebuilding. The conclusion is only that the government itself shouldn't help.
B. This contradicts the argument. We know the community is determined to rebuild. So according to this principle, the government should help. But the argument's conclusion was that the government should *not* help.
C. This has no effect. The community *is* committed, so they meet the necessary condition for government assistance. So this can't prove that the government should not assist.
D. **CORRECT.** This proves the conclusion. We know that there is a risk of serious injury from landslides. This tells us that the government therefore shouldn't assist in trail building.
E. The stimulus did *not* say the government should discourage the residents from building the trail. Instead, the conclusion is merely that the government itself shouldn't build a trail.

Question 6

QUESTION TYPE: Necessary Assumption

CONCLUSION: Climate change is an opportunity.

REASONING: If human behavior causes climate change, then we can control climate change to make it less extreme.

ANALYSIS: This argument has a bit of a different structure from most. The right answer actually points out the weakness of a premise itself. This is rare on the LSAT, but not impossible. The faulty premise is that, if we cause climate change, then we can control the climate to make it better.

The right answer points out that we might not be able to control our own behavior. If we can't control our behavior, we can't control the climate. So this answer directly contradicts the premise.

A. It doesn't matter whether the cause of climate change influences the severity of the effects. The issue is whether we can *control* climate change.
Negation: Human and natural climate change both have similar effects.
B. **CORRECT.** The negation of this destroys the premise that we can control climate change. If we can't control our behavior, we can't control climate change.
Negation: Humans are incapable of controlling the behavior that affects climate change.
C. It doesn't matter what happened in the past. There's a first time for everything.
Negation: This is the first time that humans have affected the climate.
D. It doesn't matter who is at risk from climate change. If we can control climate change, we can reduce the risks.
Negation: Other species face just as much risk from climate change as humans do.
E. It almost never matters if one thing is easier/larger/more important than another thing. Do you care if LSAT or GPA is more important for law school admissions? They're both rather important, and the relative rank won't affect any decisions you make.
Negation: It is equally easy to identify and to change behaviors that cause climate change.

Question 7

QUESTION TYPE: Complete the Argument

CONCLUSION: Stress can decrease pain.

REASONING: Patients who are waiting in uncertainty for treatment are less likely to experience pain. Uncertainty is stressful.

ANALYSIS: Note that *every* patient is waiting for some kind of treatment. If patients don't need surgery, they'll get something else. This wait is stressful. But oddly, the stressed group has less pain. The only thing we can conclude is that stress somehow reduces pain.

Common sense and science tell us that stress doesn't reduce pain. Normally, the LSAT doesn't contradict common sense. But here, the right answer does. Common sense is a useful guide, but you must ignore it when it contradicts the question.

Note that the high pain group hasn't been selected for surgery. Instead, they merely know what treatment they'll get, which could include non-surgical treatments.

A. **CORRECT.** This is the best answer. The only differences between the groups are that one knows what treatment they'll receive, and the other doesn't. The high uncertainty group has more stress but less pain, so it's reasonable to say that the stress must be reducing pain.
B. All we know about the high pain group is that they know what treatment they're getting. But we can't say they have this knowledge *because* they're in pain, so there's no clear benefit.
C. Not so. The group that didn't receive information had a *lower* rate of pain. It seems like their condition was better, not worse.
D. Hard to say. The passage never says what causes reduced blood flow to the heart. Stress could well be a cause, and also an effect.
E. This was very tempting. But the stimulus didn't say that the high pain group was receiving surgery! It instead said the high pain group knew what treatment they would receive. That could include drugs or some other therapy. So we have no information about surgery itself.

Question 8

QUESTION TYPE: Flawed Reasoning

CONCLUSION: Kodiak bears instinctively know how to walk on their hind legs. They don't need to learn.

REASONING: The shape of Kodiak bear hip and feet bones make it natural for the bears to stand on their hind legs.

ANALYSIS: This is a very bad argument. Humans are suited to walking upright, but we still have to learn. Walking isn't quite an instinct with us. Something can be both innate and learned.

A. The argument doesn't mention any specific bears. Instead, it talks about the bones of the bear population as a whole.
   Example of flaw: This Kodiak bear had an enormous nose. So all Kodiak bears must have enormous noses.
B. **CORRECT.** In real life there's often no "either/or". A lot of things have multiple causes. It's possible that Kodiak bears have the innate structure to walk on their hind legs, but they also need to learn to do so.
C. I checked my dictionary. "Behavior" only really has one definition. There answer could *never* be true for the word "behavior". If you pick an answer that says a definition changed, you need to be *very* sure what the two different definitions are.
   Example of flaw: Glasses are useful for drinking, so these reading glasses I got from my optometrist must be useful for drinking.
D. The argument wasn't talking about all behavior. The author only gave an opinion about Kodiak bears. This answer doesn't accurately describe the argument.
   Example of flaw: I believe that all behavior can only be described in one or both of two ways. I have no evidence for this claim.
E. There was no appeal to authority.
   Example of flaw: My uncle Bob said Kodiak bears walk by instinct. He's smart, so he must be right.

Question 9

QUESTION TYPE: Paradox

PARADOX: People are interested in anecdotes, not statistics. Anecdotes are inaccurate. Yet people's statistical beliefs are usually accurate.

ANALYSIS: The questions says that we like anecdotes. However, the question doesn't say that we change our beliefs based on anecdotes.

We might just like listening to anecdotes, and being emotionally moved by them. But that doesn't mean they're how we form beliefs about society. Small distinctions like this are crucial on the LSAT.

This is a hard question. The right answer doesn't fully resolve the paradox: we still don't know how people form accurate beliefs about society if they rarely pay attention to statistics.

A. This statement is often *true,* but you're not looking for an answer that's true. You want something that resolves the paradox above.
B. **CORRECT.** The stimulus said that we're moved by anecdotes, but it didn't actually say that we change our beliefs based on them. This answer suggests people don't use anecdotes to determine their beliefs. So this reduces the chance we use misleading anecdotes to form our beliefs about society.
C. This doesn't explain anything. If an anecdote is both compelling and misleading, then people would get the wrong beliefs. But the stimulus says that people largely have correct beliefs.
D. This doesn't tell us that statistics actually influence us. Whether or not statistics are comprehensible, the stimulus said we ignore them.
E. This doesn't tell us anything about statistics or anecdotes. It's just a statement about how people react to other people. That doesn't help – we're trying to find out how people form beliefs about society.

LSAT 74 – SECTION IV, LR

Question 10

QUESTION TYPE: Argument Evaluation

CONCLUSION: Schweitzer's research helps show that dinosaurs are related to birds.

REASONING: Mary Schweitzer found that the collagen in *Tyrannosaurus Rex* is similar to that found in chickens.

ANALYSIS: This argument sounds very persuasive, but it hasn't told us much.

Sure, *T. Rex* collagen is like chicken collagen. But is *T. Rex* collagen *different* from mammal collagen? Maybe all collagen is alike. In that case, the similarity between *T. Rex* and chickens proves nothing.

To evaluate the argument, we should know if related species are more likely to have similar collagen.

A. Who cares how hard it was to find tissue. *We found some.* The argument is about whether this soft tissue lets us prove anything.
B. Not relevant. Any complicated claim will have *some* evidence against it.
   Also, the conclusion is not that *T. Rex* is related to birds. Rather, the conclusion is that Schweitzer's evidence *helps prove* that dinosaurs and birds are related.
C. **CORRECT.** This is very relevant. If unrelated animals also tend to have identical collagen, then Schweitzer's evidence is meaningless.
D. Who cares? Consider this hypothetical:
   * *T. Rex* is 95% related to most dinosaurs.
   * *T. Rex* is 90% related to chickens.
   * *T. Rex is* 89% related to one unusual species of dinosaur.
   * *T. Rex* is only 70% related to mammals.
   In this hypothetical *T. Rex* is more closely related to chickens than one unusual dinosaur species. But what does that prove? *T. Rex* is still more closely related to that dinosaur than to animals that are neither dinosaur nor bird (such as mammals).
E. It doesn't matter what researchers thought beforehand. The results are all that matter.

Question 11

QUESTION TYPE: Most Strongly Supported

FACTS:
- A professor was sleep deprived when lecturing.
- She felt very tired and ineffective.
- The students didn't notice the difference.

ANALYSIS: We often notice small changes in ourselves far more than outsiders do. That's the moral here.

There's not really anything more to this question. Your job on a question like this is just to condense the stimulus down to a more manageable form, like I've done above.

A. **CORRECT.** This answer uses fancy words. Don't skip over answers without trying to understand hard words from context. Start with words you know, and use them to deduce the meaning of other words.
   This answer just means: Sleep deprivation makes you feel different, but others hardly notice a change.
B. This isn't true. It's possible the students had the more accurate view. The professor felt very different, but she may not actually have been very different.
C. We don't know if the differences in the professor's behavior were typical of all professors, and we don't know how this compares to other professions.
D. This doesn't matter. The stimulus was only talking about occasional sleep deprivation (when the professor worked in the lab all night).
E. Actually, we don't know. The students say they saw few effects, but we have no idea if their testimony is accurate or not.

Question 12

QUESTION TYPE: Principle – Paradox

PARADOX:

- All people are equal.
- Yet it's somehow more important to satisfy the people of our country.

ANALYSIS: This is both a paradox question and a principle question. We only know the two things above.

The only way to resolve this dilemma is to have a principle that somehow says countries should satisfy their own needs first.

———————

A. This tells us when *not* to satisfy needs. We're trying to show that the country *should* satisfy its own needs.
B. This gives us a *necessary* condition for satisfying your own country's needs. That's useless. It doesn't help prove that the country *should* satisfy its own needs.
C. This doesn't help. The stimulus says that all people's needs are objectively the same. So this principle doesn't let us give priority to one group over the other.
D. **CORRECT.** The stimulus says that everyone's needs are equally important. This principle tells us what to do in that case: governments should satisfy the needs of their own people.
E. This is useless. We don't know if there are no other ways for a country's people's needs to be satisfied, so this principle doesn't do anything.

Question 13

QUESTION TYPE: Must be True

FACTS:

- All neighborhoods will be cleaned at least once a month.
- If a neighborhood needs more sweeping, then it will be eligible for interim sweeps.
- Any eligible interim sweep requests will be met right away.

ANALYSIS: This question is pretty straightforward. But there are a few potential points of confusion.

1. The first sentence strongly implies that there is a fixed monthly cleaning that happens in every neighborhood, regardless of additional requests. "Interim" also implies this: it means "in between", as in "in between regular sweepings".
2. Any qualified neighborhood can get more sweepings. But that doesn't mean that *only* qualified neighborhoods get more sweepings. There might be other reasons a neighborhood could be granted an additional sweeping.

So every neighborhood has one regular sweeping. If they're qualified, they get as many interim sweepings as they want. And the stimulus didn't exclude the possibility that neighborhoods can get extra sweepings even if they aren't qualified.

———————

A. Not true. The stimulus mentions construction *that leaves dirt.* Construction might not qualify a neighborhood if there is no dirt.
B. Not so. The stimulus said that qualified neighborhoods will get additional sweepings *if they request them.* If there's no request, qualified neighborhoods might only be swept once.
C. Not true. Qualification is one justification for getting an additional sweeping, but there could be other reasons for multiple sweepings.
D. **CORRECT.** This is true. Every neighborhood gets a regular monthly sweeping. And qualified neighborhoods will get a second, interim sweep *immediately* if they request one.
E. This is almost exactly the same as answer C. They can't both be right. This is wrong because the stimulus didn't say that *only* qualified neighborhoods can get extra sweepings.

Question 14

QUESTION TYPE: Method of Reasoning

CONCLUSION: It's wrong to say that withholding information is as bad as lying.

REASONING: Lying gives people wrong beliefs. Withholding information only allows a new false belief to form.

ANALYSIS: The journalist makes a somewhat valid distinction. Withholding info does seem less bad than outright lying.

The method of argument is to show a distinction between two concepts and show that one (withholding info) is ok based on that distinction.

A. **CORRECT.** This matches. See especially the sentence that starts with "however". The journalist says that critics fail to see the difference between lying and merely withholding information. Both are similar, but this key difference means only lying is wrong.

B. Not so. This describes a situation where others are *attacking* a distinction. But in this argument, the author is criticizing those who *didn't see a distinction at all*. The author makes a new argument that there is a distinction that everyone missed.

C. The journalist defines *two* terms: lying, and withholding information.

D. Gad, this is complex. It has nothing to do with the passage. I've made a parallel argument below to show what this answer *would* look like.
Example of answer: You say it's always right to tell the truth. This therefore proves you should have handed your brother over to the police. But in some cases, the truth can kill people from shock. For instance, my uncle Harris died when he learned his son gained his fortune by fraud. Therefore, the truth is not always good, and that principle cannot support your argument that you should turn in your brother.

E. The journalist didn't give examples of when withholding information is allowed and when it isn't. So there was no clarification of this moral principle by examples.

Question 15

QUESTION TYPE: Flawed Reasoning

CONCLUSION: There's no argument for lowering interest rates.

REASONING: One reason for lowering interest rates isn't valid.

ANALYSIS: The economist has shown that we don't need to lower interest rates in order to stimulate economic growth. The flaw is that the economist ignores other possible reasons for lowering interest rates.

For this argument to have been correct, the economist would have had to say "and there are no other reasons for lowering interest rates".

A. The economist didn't cite any experts to support her argument. Instead, she *disagreed* with other expert economists.

B. This didn't happen.
Example of flaw: Lower interest rates can stimulate economic growth. Therefore, lower interest rates *are* economic growth. Any lowering of interest rates will always make us richer, and the country with the lowest rates will grow richest fastest.

C. **CORRECT.** If there are other reasons to lower interest rates, then the economist's argument is badly incomplete.

D. The economist didn't say that lower interest rates are the *only* way to stimulate economic growth.

E. This is a tempting answer. But the economist didn't say that lowering interest rates will push the economy into unsustainable growth. Instead, the economist merely argued that lower interest rates aren't needed. They might believe that a further lowering of interest rates would have no effect, since the economy is already growing.

Question 16

QUESTION TYPE: Sufficient Assumption

CONCLUSION: Either the commentators are wrong, or Mather's definition of Baroque is wrong.

REASONING: The commentators think Caravaggio was Baroque. Mather thinks Baroque paintings must be opulent, extravagant, with heroic sweep.

ANALYSIS: This argument makes a *really* big error. The author never said whether Caravaggio's paintings had opulence, extravagance and heroic sweep! If Caravaggio had all those things, then the commentators could be right in classifying him as Baroque, and this would match Mather's definition. To prove that either the commentators or Mather are wrong, we need to show that Caravaggio's paintings lacked those qualities.

Note that E is pretty obviously correct. The first four answers are designed to confuse you and slow you down so you waste 30 seconds before you even read E. Look over all of the answers first before considering any of them at length.

A. This answer doesn't apply to the stimulus. We don't care what's typically true. We only care about the specific attributes Mather mentioned, and whether Caravaggio's paintings had them. This is a useless, wishy-washy answer. The only purpose of an answer like this is to slow you down and keep you from seeing that E is obviously correct.
B. The stimulus isn't about how to define a realistic painting. This answer can't lead to the conclusion. This is just here to confuse you.
C. The past doesn't matter. This argument is only talking about Caravaggio, and Baroque, which was in Caravaggio's future.
D. This is close, but we don't care what "usually" happens in realistic paintings. Caravaggio's paintings might have been unusual in that they were both realistic but also heroic, opulent and extravagant.
E. CORRECT. If this is true, then the paintings aren't Baroque, according to Mather. Yet the commentators say Caravaggio was Baroque. So either they or Mather are wrong.

Question 17

QUESTION TYPE: Method of Reasoning

CONCLUSION: Jury nullification is a bad idea.

REASONING: Juries often make serious mistakes when they can nullify a conviction if they think it's unfair.

ANALYSIS: The argument says that jury nullification is intrinsically flawed. It fails because nullification relies on jurors being objective. Since jurors aren't objective, they make mistakes.

A. The argument didn't do this.
Example of method: Jury proponents are fat capitalist oppressors. Therefore they are wrong.
B. This is tempting. But an inconsistency is a precise thing. It's when two statements *literally* contradict each other. That didn't happen.
Example of flaw: The proponents of jury nullification say that it will frequently avoid serious injustices, and they also argue that we shouldn't worry about it because nullification isn't used very much. But this is inconsistent: If jury nullification isn't used much, then it can't frequently avoid injustice.
C. This didn't happen.
Example of method: The proponents of jury nullification say that it only rarely leads to mistakes. But when we analyzed 1000 cases of nullification, 200 of them were mistaken.
D. This didn't happen.
Example of method: The proponents of jury nullification say that it never leads to serious error. But in the Roberts case, the jury let a murderer go free, and then he killed three more people.
E. CORRECT. The undesirable consequences are the serious mistakes that nullification can lead to.

Question 18

QUESTION TYPE: Flawed Reasoning

CONCLUSION: It's true that older people's pineal glands produces less melatonin.

REASONING: People aged 65-81 who take melatonin have less insomnia. Melatonin helps you sleep.

ANALYSIS: This argument has *two* major flaws. First, this is a classic example of a false comparison. The argument didn't tell us anything about people who are younger than 65!

If melatonin *also* helps young people sleep, then we can't say that older people produce less melatonin. Maybe melatonin deficiencies are common in all ages.

The second flaw is a biased sample. The study only looked at older people *who already have insomnia*. We don't know anything about older people who sleep well. Maybe most people aged 65-81 have more than enough melatonin and supplementation wouldn't help them sleep.

By the way, melatonin disruption is a serious issue. The bright blue lights of our computers and phones late at night prevent melatonin production. You can reduce this issue by installing f.lux on your computer. On Android, use Twilight. On iPhone, there is no solution, but you can install f.lux if your phone is jailbroken.

Flux: https://justgetflux.com/
Android: https://play.google.com/store/apps/details?id=com.urbandroid.lux&hl=en

Thank me later.

A. This didn't happen.
   Example of flaw: You spilled water on your computer, and it broke. Therefore, you intended to break your computer.
B. This didn't happen. It's true that melatonin manufacturers made a claim, but the argument didn't use evidence from the melatonin manufacturers to support the claim.
   Example of flaw: Melatonin manufacturers have produced a study that says we should take melatonin. Therefore we should take melatonin.
C. This didn't happen.
   Example of flaw: Melatonin plays a role in our biological clock. So melatonin must affect that mechanical grandfather clock in the hallway.
D. This didn't happen.
   Example of flaw: He won the lottery, and he's happy now. So happiness must lead to lottery victories. If I am happy, I'll win.
E. **CORRECT.** The study only looked at older people *who have insomnia*. It makes sense that people with insomnia have less melatonin. But we don't know if most people who are aged 65-81 have low melatonin production. Maybe melatonin has little to no effect for most people of that age.

Question 19

QUESTION TYPE: Parallel Reasoning

CONCLUSION: The concert probably had bad promotion.

REASONING: Wells is an expert on concerts. Wells thought the concert would sell out unless the promotion wasn't good. The concert didn't sell out.

ANALYSIS: This is a good argument. It's an example of how to properly cite a relevant authority.

Wells gives the following conditional statement: ~~sell out~~ → Poorly promoted

We have the sufficient condition – the concert didn't sell out. So according to Wells, the concert must have been poorly promoted.

The conclusion only says the concert "probably" was poorly promoted. Why? Wells is an expert, so we can say his opinion is worth something. But it's also not certain Wells is right. So we have some reason for believing there was poor promotion, but also room for doubt. Therefore, the argument says: probably.

To match this argument, look for:

1. A conditional statement from a qualified expert.
2. The sufficient condition of the conditional.
3. A conclusion that says "probably" or a synonym.

Parallel reasoning questions are *long*. You must learn how to skim the answers. Using the three elements above, you can soft eliminate several wrong answers. If an answer deviates from the script, it's almost certainly not correct.

I say "soft eliminate" because it's easy to make a mistake. You don't want to say an answer is certainly wrong. And if you're not sure an answer is disqualified, don't eliminate it. But on your first pass, focus on taking answers out of the running using the list above.

A. Dr. Smith, the heart surgeon, didn't give a conditional statement. They said the patient would "probably" survive. That's a "most" statement.
   In the stimulus, Wells said the concert would *definitely* sell out if the promotion were good. Only the conclusion said "probably".
B. Professor Willis didn't give a conditional. She just said "probably". This doesn't match the stimulus: Wells gave a condition statement, and only the *conclusion* said probably.
C. **CORRECT.** This matches exactly. Expert says:
   Damage → ~~Properly Repaired~~
   The argument gives the sufficient condition (damage) and concludes that the necessary condition "probably" occurred. This shows we should trust the expert to some degree, but not take their word as gospel.
D. This answer concludes that the expert builder is wrong. But in the stimulus, the author thinks Wells is right!
E. This answer gets the conditional backwards. The evidence is: properly conducted → lead. The argument goes backwards, incorrectly, from finding lead to properly conducted. It's possible lead was found even though the tests were botched.

Question 20

QUESTION TYPE: Flawed Reasoning

CONCLUSION: We can never stop global recessions.

REASONING: To stop recessions, we'd need to predict them. But currently, we can't predict them.

ANALYSIS: This argument confuses the future with the present. It's true that we *currently* can't predict recessions, and therefore we can't stop them.

But at some point, economists might get better at predicting. Then perhaps we could predict recessions and therefore prevent recessions.

You might have thought the flaw was that someone else could predict recessions, other than economists. That could have been an answer, but it was unlikely for two reasons: Economists are the relevant experts, and they're also using the best techniques.

A. This is circular reasoning. Circular reasoning is rarely the flaw, but it often appears in the answers.
   Example of flaw: Recessions can't be stopped because they're unstoppable.
B. It doesn't matter what economists claim. It only matters what they're able to do.
C. This answer describes confusing a necessary condition for a sufficient condition. But the author didn't say that recessions could definitely be stopped if they were predictable.
D. **CORRECT.** If techniques significantly improve, then economists might be able to predict recessions.
E. This is a different flaw.
   Example of flaw: We can't know when a recession will happen. So recessions will never happen.

Question 21

QUESTION TYPE: Principle

CONCLUSION: The newspaper is incorrectly biased against the possibility of spaceships.

REASONING: The newspaper was skeptical of Mr. Hanlon's claim that he saw a UFO. But if Mr. Hanlon had claimed to see a natural phenomenon, the newspaper wouldn't have been skeptical, because Mr. Hanlon is trusted by the community.

ANALYSIS: You're looking for something that contradicts the argument. From the letter to the editor, we know that the report was published, so that's not at issue.

The complaint is that the newspaper was unduly biased against the claim of UFOs. The right answer must therefore talk about bias or skepticism.

A. **CORRECT.** This principle suggests the newspaper should have been skeptical unless Mr. Hanlon had extraordinary evidence. As far as we know, Mr. Hanlon had no such evidence. Since we have no proof that Mr. Hanlon met the necessary condition, this principle suggests that the paper was right to be skeptical of Mr. Hanlon.
B. There's no claim coming from an intermediary source. Mr. Hanlon appears to have spoken directly to the newspaper.
C. This *supports* the argument. It's a principle the letter's author agrees with. We're looking for a principle that *contradicts* the argument.
D. This principle tells us what *Mr. Hanlon* should have done. But the argument is about what the *newspaper* should have done.
E. This is tempting. But the argument was about *bias,* not whether the newspaper should have published at all.
   So while the author of the letter to the editor might disagree with this principle, this completely fails to address the argument in the letter. The letter's argument was about how to *present* a report once it is published.

Question 22

QUESTION TYPE: Flawed Reasoning

CONCLUSION: The specialized algae scraping ability evolved more than once.

REASONING: One possible sufficient condition for single evolution didn't happen.

ANALYSIS: This is a very bad argument. It talks about fish that live in Blue Lake and Flower Lake. The argument presents this single conditional statement:

closely related → evolved once

The argument then negates the sufficient condition: scientists have shown that the fish aren't closely related.

But negating the sufficient doesn't negate the necessary. It's perhaps possible that the ability evolved only once even though the fish aren't closely related. Perhaps the fish are loosely related.

A. This is a different flaw.
   Example of flaw: Algae-scraping is correlated with the two lakes. So the two lakes must have caused the algae scraping ability.
B. This is a different flaw.
   Example of flaw: John says he will get the job. But since we don't know if that's true yet, clearly John will not get the job.
C. **CORRECT.** This is it. See the analysis above. The author assumed that being closely related was a necessary condition for single evolution.
D. This is a different flaw.
   Example of flaw: Algae scraping fish will probably go extinct soon. So they definitely will go extinct soon, with 100% certainty.
E. This is a different flaw. For this to be correct, we'd need to know there was some reason to suspect that the opinion of the biologists was not universal. Here, we have no reason to believe that other biologists would disagree.
   Example of flaw: Dr. Jones, famous for his disagreements with the biological community, believes that the algae-scraping ability evolved many times. So Jones must be right.

Question 23

QUESTION TYPE: Principle

PRINCIPLES:
- The country must sell state owned entities for the highest price possible.
- The country must make sure that citizens of Country F are the majority owners for at least a year after the sale.

ANALYSIS: The setup itself is confusing. Once you understand it clearly, the answers are a lot easier.

The constitution of Country F gives the government two conflicting requirements. It has to sell the entity for the highest price it can get. And it has to make sure citizens still own most of the new company.

How is this a conflict? Suppose foreigners are offering a higher price for shares of the entity. In that case, the government would have to choose between accepting a lower price from citizens or allowing majority foreign ownership.

To be clear: the governments is not required to own any part of the entity after sale. Instead, it's required to make sure that *private citizens* of country F have majority ownership of the new company.

A. A minority share of StateAir by non-citizens is fine. This situation violates no rules.
B. It doesn't matter where operations take place. It only matters where the new owners of National Silver live. The majority of the shares will be owned by citizens, so this is fine.
C. The question is asking which situation *necessarily* violates a rule. Here, World Oil Company has made "one of" the highest offers for PetroNat. But that doesn't matter: the government has to accept the *highest* offer. We don't know if the highest offer is foreign or domestic, so we can't say that this situation must lead to a violation.
D. The highest bid for National Telephone is fine. Citizens own a majority of the shares.
E. **CORRECT.** This leads to a violation. Either the government will get a lower price, or foreigners will own most of StateRail.

Question 24

QUESTION TYPE: Weaken

CONCLUSION: Activite must work.

REASONING: If you buy Activite, you'll get an extra month's supply for free.

ANALYSIS: This question is rather confusing. I think it may be flawed by ambiguity. I'm going to break from my usual style and start by discussing the right answer, D. It says that the shipping fee is much more than the cost of making and shipping product.

This does weaken the argument, but it's not clear exactly how the situation plays out. This is unusual for an LSAT question, and it makes it difficult to predict the answer or think clearly about the situation in order to critique it. I can see at least three possibilities. I've sketched them out below.

I *think* the situation is as follows:

- You buy Activite. You don't pay for the first month's product. It's free.
- (As per answer D) However, you pay the regular handling fee.

Another possible situation is this:

- You buy Activite, and pay for it.
- The makers will therefore also send you a free extra month's supply.
- (according to answer D) You'll also be charged a heavy handling fee for the free product.

A third possible situation is this:

- You buy Activite. You get a regular supply + an extra month's supply. Both are shipped in the same package.
- It's not much more expensive to pack and ship the second package along with the first. Neither the product nor shipping costs much.
- The handling fee covers the cost of both sets.

In all situations, the handling fee covers the cost of the extra product.

A. This answer is trying to show that Activite isn't *necessary*. But that's not the point of the argument. The point of the argument is that it is *useful*. A lot of people don't eat balanced diets, so perhaps they could benefit from Activite.

B. The argument isn't about whether Activite is the *best* option. It's only about whether Activite works. For the purposes of the argument, it wouldn't matter if Activite cost $1 billion, as long as it worked.

C. This just says "most" dietary supplements. That might not include Activite. This answer is useless.

D. CORRECT. If this is true, then Activite is still making a profit even on the free offers. Therefore, they could afford this strategy even if the product didn't work and no one reordered.

E. This statement is true, but we're not looking for something that is true. This answer doesn't mean that Activite has harmful side effects. And Activite might be effective even if it had some side effects. Most drugs have side effects, but we consider them to be effective drugs nonetheless.

Question 25

QUESTION TYPE: Flawed Parallel Reasoning

CONCLUSION: If you dislike the Prime Minister, it's probably because you dislike her plan to raise income tax.

REASONING: Teresa wants the income tax to be raised. So she probably likes the Prime Minister.

ANALYSIS: This is a bad argument. People are complicated, and our political opinions don't all fall in a line. Theresa might like income tax increases, but dislike the Prime Minister for some other reason.

The argument incorrectly tries to take the contrapositive of this "most" statement:

Dislike PM (most)→ dislike income tax plan

The argument reverses and negates the terms above. This doesn't work for "most" statements the way it does for normal conditional statements. "Most" people who dislike the Prime Minister do so because of taxes, but some people, like Theresa, might dislike the PM for other reasons.

The wrong answers fit into two groups. B and C say that the person in question fails to match the *left* side of the "most" statement. But in the stimulus, Theresa failed to match the *right* side of the "most" statement.

D and E are good arguments. "Most" is the same as "probably". If most cats are black, then it's correct to say that an individual cat is "probably" black. If we know nothing else about the cat, then the general "most" statement applies directly. So if 54% of cats are black, then an individual cat has a 54% chance of being black. Both D and E correctly apply individual cases to "most" statements in this way.

A. **CORRECT.** This matches. There is a "most" statement, and the argument incorrectly tries to take the contrapositive of that statement: Support logging (most)→ believe in risk of fires

Andy doesn't believe in the risk of fires, but that doesn't mean he supports logging. We only know that *most* people who support logging believe in fires. But some people, like Andy, might support logging for other reasons.

B. This doesn't work. In the stimulus, Theresa wasn't part of the *right hand side* of the "most" statement. Here, Bonnie isn't part of the *left hand side* of the "most" statement (expecting population to increase over the next ten years).

C. Same as B. In the stimulus, Theresa wasn't part of the *right hand side* of the "most" statement. Here, Chung isn't part of the *left hand side* of the most statement (believing the economy improved).

D. This is a good argument.
Oppose Loffoch Valley light rail feasibility study (most)→ support valley freeway.
This correctly applies Donna's situation to the "most" statement. Donna opposes the study, so it's true to say that she probably supports the freeway.

E. This is a good argument.
Believe blizzard tomorrow (most)→ Channel 9 news
Eddies believes there will be a blizzard, so it's correct to apply the "most" statement to him and say he probably saw the news report.

Question 26

QUESTION TYPE: Strengthen

CONCLUSION: There are fewer mourning doves because there is less nesting habitat for them in the area.

REASONING: Mourning doves used to nest in orchards until sprinklers were installed.

ANALYSIS: This argument makes a causation-correlation error. True, the mourning dove decline happened at the same time that the sprinklers were installed. But that doesn't mean that the habitat decline *caused* the decrease of doves in the area. There could have been other, more important reasons: less food, more predators, new food supply in a different area, etc.

The argument has also failed to show that the loss of the orchard truly was a problem for the mourning doves. If there was still much available habitat in the area, then loss of the orchard likely wasn't the cause. Answer B addresses this by showing that the orchard was the only suitable habitat.

You might have thought "maybe the sprinklers didn't truly ruin the orchard as habitat". This is possible, but unlikely – sprinklers are pretty disruptive. Answer C does address this possibility by showing that the sprinklers were indeed a problem. If B didn't exist, I would have chosen C. But B is a far stronger answer. It's rare for there to be two answers that strengthen an argument, but this question shows that it's possible. In such cases, you should follow the question stem's direction: you're choosing the answer that *most* strengthens the argument.

A. This *weakens* the argument by providing an alternate cause. If mourning doves can now be hunted, then maybe hunting is the cause of the decline.

B. CORRECT. This strengthens the argument by increasing the impact of the sprinklers. The sprinklers affected the doves' *only* habitat.

C. I think this answer does slightly strengthen the argument, by confirming that the sprinklers ruined the orchard as a habitat. But it's not much of a strengthen. It's already pretty reasonable to assume that sprinklers ruin trees as a habitat. Further, this doesn't show that the doves actually lacked habitat in the area. If other trees were suitable, then loss of the orchard wouldn't have been a big deal. Only B shows that the orchard was a critical habitat.

D. This doesn't have any impact. Only a *change* would have reduced the number of morning doves. This answer doesn't say that residents *changed* what they put in their feeders.

E. This is too vague to be useful. We already knew that the doves nested in apple trees. This just tells us doves often nest in fruit trees. But it doesn't mean that *only* apple trees make good habitats for doves. This actually weakens the argument slightly by showing that other fruit trees in the area might have made good replacement habitats.

Appendix: LR Questions By Type

Strengthen

Section I, #2
Section I, #4
Section I, #17
Section IV, #3
Section IV, #5
Section IV, #26

Weaken

Section I, #6
Section I, #23
Section IV, #24

Sufficient Assumption

Section I, #12
Section I, #20
Section IV, #16

Parallel Reasoning

Section I, #19
Section IV, #19

Flawed Parallel Reasoning

Section I, #25
Section IV, #25

Necessary Assumption

Section I, #8
Section IV, #4
Section IV, #6

Method of Reasoning

Section IV, #14
Section IV, #17

Must Be True

Section I, #24
Section IV, #24

Most Strongly Supported

Section I, #11
Section I, #22
Section IV, #11

Paradox

Section I, #9
Section I, #15
Section IV, #9
Section IV, #12 (Also principle)

Principle

Section I, #3
Section I, #7
Section I, #10
Section IV, #5
Section IV, #12 (Also paradox)
Section IV, #21
Section IV, #23

Identify The Conclusion

Section I, #13
Section IV, #2

Argument Evaluation

Section I, #21
Section IV, #10

Complete the Argument

Section I, #1
Section IV, #7

Role in Argument

Section I, #14

Misinterpretation

Section IV, #1

Flawed Reasoning

Section I, #5
Section I, #16
Section I, #18
Section IV, #8
Section IV, #15
Section IV, #18
Section IV, #20
Section IV, #22

Thank You

First of all, thank you for buying this book. Writing these explanations has been the most satisfying work I have ever done. I sincerely hope they have been helpful to you, and I wish you success on the LSAT and as a lawyer.

If you left an Amazon review, you get an extra special thank you! I truly appreciate it. You're helping others discover LSAT Hacks.

Thanks also to Anu Panil, who drew the diagrams for the logic games. Anu, thank you for making sense of the scribbles and scans I sent you. You are surely ready to master logic games after all the work you did.

Thanks to Alison Rayner, who helped me with the layout and designed the cover. If this book looks nice, she deserves credit. Alison caught many mistakes I would never have found by myself (any that remain are my own, of course).

Thanks to Ludovic Glorieux, who put up with me constantly asking him if a design change looked good or bad.

Finally, thanks to my parents, who remained broadly supportive despite me being crazy enough to leave law school to teach the LSAT. I love you guys.

About The Author

Graeme Blake lives in Montreal Canada. He first took the LSAT in June 2007, and scored a 177. It was love at first sight. He taught the LSAT for Testmasters for a couple of years before going to the University of Toronto for law school.

Upon discovering that law was not for him, Graeme began working as an independent LSAT tutor. He teaches LSAT courses in Montreal for Ivy Global and tutors students from all around the world using Skype.

He publishes a series of LSAT guides and explanations under the title LSAT Hacks. Versions of these explanations can be found at LSAT Blog, Cambridge LSAT and LSAT Hacks, as well as amazon.com.

Graeme is also the moderator of www.reddit.com/r/LSAT, Reddit's LSAT forum. He worked for a time with 7Sage LSAT.

Graeme finds it unusual to write in the third person to describe himself, but he recognizes the importance of upholding publishing traditions. He wonders if many people read about the author pages.

You can find him at www.lsathacks.com and www.reddit.com/r/LSAT.

Graeme encourages you to get in touch by email, his address is graeme@lsathacks.com. Or you can call 514-612-1526. He's happy to hear feedback or give advice.

Further Reading

I hope you liked this book. If you did, I'd be very grateful if you took two minutes to review it on amazon. People judge a book by its reviews, and if you review this book you'll help other LSAT students discover it.

Ok, so you've written a review and want to know what to do next.

The most important LSAT books are the preptests themselves. Many students think they have to read every strategy guide under the sun, but you'll learn the most simply from doing real LSAT questions and analyzing your mistakes.

At the time of writing, there are 74 official LSATs. The most recent ones are best, but if you've got a while to study I recommend doing every test from 19 or from 29 onwards.

This series (LSAT Hacks) is a bit different from other LSAT prep books. This book is not a strategy guide.

Instead, my goal is to let you do what my own students get to do when they take lessons with me: review their work with the help of an expert.

These explanations show you a better way to approach questions, and exactly why answers are right or wrong.

If you found this book useful, here's the list of other books in the series:

(Note – the series was formerly titled "Hacking the LSAT" so the older books still have that title until I update them)

- Hacking The LSAT: Full Explanations For LSATs 29-38, Volume I
- Hacking The LSAT: Full Explanations For LSATs 29-38, Volume II
- LSAT 62 Explanations (Hacking The LSAT Series)
- LSAT 63 Explanations (Hacking The LSAT Series)
- LSAT 64 Explanations (Hacking The LSAT Series)
- LSAT 65 Explanations (Hacking The LSAT Series)
- LSAT 66 Explanations (Hacking The LSAT Series)
- LSAT 67 Explanations (Hacking The LSAT Series)
- LSAT 68 Explanations (Hacking The LSAT Series)
- LSAT 69 Explanations (Hacking The LSAT Series)
- LSAT 70 Explanations (Hacking The LSAT Series)
- LSAT 71 Explanations (Hacking The LSAT Series)
- LSAT 72 Explanations (LSAT Hacks Series)
- LSAT 73 Explanations (LSAT Hacks Series)
- LSAT 74 Explanations (LSAT Hacks Series)

Keep an eye out, as I'll be steadily publishing explanations for other LSATs.

If you *are* looking for strategy guides, try Manhattan LSAT or Powerscore. Unlike other companies, they use real LSAT questions in their books.

I've written a longer piece on LSAT books on Reddit. It includes links to the best LSAT books and preptests. If you're serious about the LSAT and want the best materials, I strongly recommend you read it:

http://redd.it/uf4uh

(this is a shortlink that takes you to the correct page)

Free LSAT Email Course

This book is just the beginning. It teaches you how to solve individual questions, but it's not designed to give you overall strategies for each section.

There's so much to learn about the LSAT. As a start, I've made a free, five day email course. Each day I'll send you an email teaching you what I know about a subject.

LSAT Email Course Overview

- Intro to the LSAT
- Logical Reasoning
- Logic Games
- Reading Comprehension
- How to study

What people say about the free LSAT course

These have been awesome. More please!!! - **Cailie**

Your emails are tremendously helpful. - **Matt**

Thanks for the tips! They were very helpful, and even make you feel like you studied a bit. Great insight and would love more! - **Haj**

Sign up for the free LSAT email course here

http://lsathacks.com/email-course/

p.s. I've had people say this free email course is more useful than an entire Kaplan course they took. It's 100% free. Good luck - Graeme

Made in the USA
Lexington, KY
17 August 2015